British Rail

LOCOMOTIVES

Includes HSTs

Edited by Roger Wood

LONDON

IAN ALLAN LTD

Above:
Class 47/4s Nos 47 500 *Great Western* and 47 628 *Sir Daniel Gooch*, both in green livery, pass Clink Road Junction with the 11.45 Paddington-Penzance on 23 September 1986. *Mike Bennett*

Previous page:
Class 45/1 1Co-Co1 No 45 150 is seen leaving Leicester at the head of the 10.31 Nottingham-London St Pancras parcels train on 30 May 1985. *C. J. Tuffs*

Traction Scene

The most significant development affecting BR's locomotive fleet in 1986 was the introduction of main line private owner diesels by Foster Yeoman for hauling its stone traffic over BR lines; the four Class 59 locomotives built in the USA replacing six BR freight locomotives. This may set a precedent for other major customers of Railfreight.

Continued reductions have become necessary in most of BR's 1960s Modernisation Plan locomotive classes. The modification of some locomotives of Classes 37, 47 and 86 has reduced the overall requirement and so enabled examples of most types, up to Class 47, to be withdrawn to provide essential spare parts and equipment to keep sufficient quantities of similar locomotives in traffic. Major accidents caused the unscheduled scrapping of a Class 31/4 and two Class 86 locomotives.

During 1987 the biggest change since the early 1960s will affect the locomotive fleet. Much of the overhaul work currently effected at main BREL workshops will be transferred to re-equipped Major BR Traction Depots for Cost Effective Maintenance — equipment and component exchange. These depots will draw on a new central stores at Doncaster for prompt supply of new or overhauled parts.

Any locomotives which still contain asbestos must be stripped of this insulation or withdrawn from service by the end of 1987 — this includes some of Classes 20 and 25. The forward requirement for locomotive-hauled passenger trains is quite clear, and the only significant change, for 1987, will see AC electric locomotives on Great Eastern services to Cambridge and Norwich from Liverpool Street. Further main line diesel locomotives will become surplus to requirements when the 23m 'Sprinter' diesel multiple-units now on order are delivered.

It is in the Railfreight Sector that the future requirement is less clear. On the assumption that the traffic totals show no significant change, the refurbishment of Classes 31 and 37 will continue, but how many and which variation(s) of the latter will ultimately receive this life-extension is undecided. Also to be determined is the future replacement for Class 47s, it is reliably reported that no more major modifications can be expected although this does not rule out the fitting of some more with long range fuel tanks.

More immediately it is expected that by May, Sector and possibly Sub-Sector ownership will have been determined for the full fleet. *Motive Power Monthly* will report this and all other relevant news promptly.

In this edition we have detailed special liveries applied that, in theory at least, have occasional relevance to the selection of a particular locomotive for a special duty.

There are currently three liveries which can be regarded as 'standard' for locomotives in Capital Stock:

All blue: Classes 03, 08, 09, 25, 27, 31/4, 33, 37/0*, 37/4, 45, 47/0*, 47/4, 50, 73/0, 81, 82, 83, 85.
InterCity: Classes 73/1, 86, 87, 89.
Railfreight: (Grey and red). Classes 20, 26, 31/1, 37/0*, 37/5 to 37/9, 47/0*, 47/3, 47/9, 56, 58.

*Classes 37/0 and 47/0 locomotives retaining operational steam generators are not yet part of the Railfreight sector.

Many locomotives in the InterCity and Railfreight categories are still in the old standard blue pending major overhaul. As this is not of significance to the normal operating or maintenance detailed reference in excluded here to allow inclusion of more significant data.

Class 37/0 Co-Co No 37 100 is seen leaving Carlisle on 2 July 1986 with a Euston-Stranraer parcels train. *C. J. Tuffs*

Equipment and Special Characteristics

Fittings which are standard to a Class or sub-Class are indicated in the heading. Other information is shown against each locomotive using, so far as possible, the official 'TOPS' code applicable.

B Clayton steam generator
C Stone-Vapor steam generator
D Spanner Mk III steam generator
E Buckeye coupling
G Driver/Guard (No 1/No 2 cab), communication
L Headlight fitted
M One Man Operation equipment
P Snowplough brackets (for three-part miniature snowplough)*
R Refurbished, Heavy General overhaul
S Slow Speed Control
T Radio Telephone or
Radio Electronic Token Block (Class 37) or
Public telephone on IC125 coaches
X Steam generator officially isolated

*Reliable information is not available concerning fitting and removal of snowploughs. Arrangements appear to vary from depot to depot. Only locomotives with brackets can be fitted with ploughs. See late news.

Coupling of Diesel Locomotives

Main line diesel locomotives of most classes are equipped to operate in multiple with locomotives having similar control systems. In order to distinguish locomotives which can operate in this way, a colour code symbol is used.

Type of Locomotive	*Coupling symbol*
All diesel-electric locomotives with electro-pneumatic control	★ **BLUE STAR**
Class 50 diesel-electric locomotives	■ **ORANGE SQUARE**
Class 56 and 58 locomotives	♦ **RED DIAMOND**

These are normally applied to the locomotive front, or jumper cable. Locomotives of different codes may be coupled but individually driven.

IMPORTANT NOTE
This booklet has been updated to information advised at late December 1986. The editor and publishers would welcome advice of any errors found in the booklet (sent to: The Editor, *ABC BR Locomotives*, Ian Allan Ltd at the address shown below) and whilst same will be investigated it will not be possible to enter into correspondence. Details of the full range of Ian Allan publications may be had by sending a 9"×6" stamped self addressed envelope for a current list to: Mail Order Department, Ian Allan Ltd, Coombelands House, Addlestone, Weybridge, Surrey KT15 1HY.

LOCOMOTIVE DEPOT CODES

Locomotives are based at a depot equipped to provide scheduled maintenance and all main work is effected at this depot when possible. Minor maintenance and repairs are carried out at the nearest convenient depot to the locomotive's location when required.

Depots with large special identification symbols on allocated locomotives are shown thus (*Salmon*).

Abbreviations used against depot names:

DMD: Diesel Maintenance Depot
EMD: Electric Maintenance Depot
EMUD: Electric Multiple-Unit Depot
FP: Fuelling Point
HS: Holding sidings. (Stabling point)
HSTD: High Speed Train Depot
LIP: Locomotive Inspection Point
OHLD: Overhead Line Depot
PAD: Pre-Assembly Depot
SD: Servicing Depot
TMD: Traction Maintenance Depot
T&RSMD: Traction and Rolling Stock Maintenance Depot

Code	*Rgn*	*Name*	*Classes allocated*	*Notes*
AB	SC	Aberdeen Ferryhill TMD	08/0	
AF	S	Ashford, Chart Leacon T&RSMD	08/0, 09	
AN	LM	Allerton TMD	08/0	Wheel lathe
AY	SC	Ayr TMD	08/0	
BD	LM	Birkenhead North EMUD	03, 97/7	
BE	LM	Bedford Midland	—	Locomotive stabling
BG	E	Hull (Botanic Gardens) TMD	08/0	
BH	E	Barrow Hill, (Staveley) Loco SD	08/0	
BI	S	Brighton T&RSMD	—	Locomotive stabling
BL	E	Blyth (Cambois)	—	Locomotive stabling
BN	E	Bounds Green T&RSMD	254	Locomotive light maintenance and stabling
BR	W	Bristol Bath Road TMD	08/0, 31/4, 37/0, 47/0, 47/3, 47/9, 56	
BS	LM	Bescot TMD	08/0, 20, 31/1, 31/4, 47/0, 47/3, 47/4	
BW	LM	Barrow in Furness HS	—	Locomotive fuelling and stabling
BX	LM	Buxton TMD	—	Locomotive fuelling and stabling
BY	LM	Bletchley TMD	08/0, 97/2 (Ethel)	
BZ	W	St Blazey (Par) Loco SD	08/0	
CA	E	Cambridge (Coldham Lane) TMD	08/0	Mainline locomotives stable at Cambridge station
CD	LM	Crewe DMD	08/0, 25/1, 25/2, 25/3, 47/0, 47/3, 47/4, 97/4	Wheel lathe
CE	LM	Crewe EMD	85	Classes 81-87 on acceptance tests ex-works ZC
CF	W	Cardiff Canton TMD	08/0, 37/0, 37/5, 37/7, 37/9, 47/0, 47/4, 56	Wheel lathe
CH	LM	Chester TMD	08/0	
CK	SC	Corkerhill Loco SD	—	Locomotive fuelling and stabling

Code	Rgn	Name	Classes allocated	Notes
CR	E	Colchester Loco SD	03, 08/0	
CV	LM	Coalville HS	—	Locomotive stabling
CW	LM	Cricklewood T&RSMD	08/0, 31/1, 97/7	Wheel lathe
DR	E	Doncaster TMD	08/0	Wheel lathe
DY	LM	Derby, Etches Park T&RSMD	08/0	
EC	SC	Edinburgh, Craigentinny T&RSMD	254	
ED	SC	Eastfield, Glasgow TMD *(Scottie Dog)*	08/0, 20, 27, 37/0, 37/4, 47/0, 47/4, 97/2 (Ethel)	Wheel lathe
EH	S	Eastleigh T&RSMD	08/0, 09, 33/0, 33/1	
EU	LM	Euston station	—	Electric locomotive stabling
EX	W	Exeter St Davids Loco SD	—	Locomotive stabling
FH	E	Frodingham (Scunthorpe) Loco SD	08/0	
FR	S	Fratton T&RSMD	—	Locomotive fuelling and stabling
FW	SC	Fort William Loco FP	—	Locomotive stabling
GD	E	Gateshead Greensfield TMD	03, 08/0, 37/0, 47/0, 47/4, 56	Wheel lathe
GL	W	Gloucester Loco SD	08/0, 97/6	
GM	SC	Grangemouth Loco SD	08/0	
GU	LM	Guide Bridge HS	—	Locomotive fuelling and stabling
GW	SC	Glasgow, Shields EMD *(Salmon)*	81	Wheel lathe
HA	SC	Haymarket TMD *(Castle)*	08/0, 20, 26/0, 26/1, 47/4, 47/7	Wheel lathe
HD	LM	Holyhead Loco SD	—	Locomotive fuelling and stabling
HE	E	Hornsey EMUD	87/1, 97/7	Headquarters owned locomotives
HF	W	Hereford HS	—	Locomotive stabling point
HM	E	Healey Mills TMD	08/0	
HT	E	Heaton T&RSMD	254	
HQ		BRB Headquarters (**RTC-D** Railway Technical Centre — Derby)	97/2, 97/4	Also new stock on acceptance (see also HE)
HQ		Private Owner locomotives operated on BR —		
		Brush Traction	91	
		Foster Yeoman	59	Maintained at Merehead
IL	E	Ilford Car Sheds EMD	—	Light maintenance on Class 86/2 for Great Eastern line services
IM	E	Immingham TMD	08/0, 31/1, 31/4, 37/0, 47/0, 47/3	
IP	E	Ipswich HS	—	Locomotive fuelling and stabling
IS	SC	Inverness TMD *(Stag)*	08/0, 37/0, 37/4, 47/0, 47/4	

Depot Codes

Code	*Rgn*	*Name*	*Classes allocated*	*Notes*
KD	LM	Kingmoor, Carlisle TMD	08/0, 31/1, 40, 47/0, 47/4	
KM		Kingmoor	25/9	BRB
KY	E	Knottingley TMD	08/0	
LA	W	Laira, Plymouth TMD	08/0, 37/0, 50, 253	Wheel lathe.
LE	W	Landore (Swansea) TMD	08/0, 08/9, 37/0	Diesel repair shops
LG	LM	Longsight EMD	—	Electric locomotive servicing
LN	E	Lincoln TMD	08/0	
LO	LM	Longsight (Diesel) TMD	08/0	
LR	LM	Leicester Loco SD	08/0	
MG	W	Margam FP	—	Locomotive fuelling and stabling
MH	SC	Millerhill (Edinburgh) Loco FP	—	Locomotive fuelling and stabling
	SC	Mossend yard	—	Locomotive stabling
ML	SC	Motherwell TMD *(Salmon)*	08/0, 20, 37/0	
MR	E	March TMD *(Hare)*	08/0, 31/1, 31/4, 37/0	
NC	E	Norwich, Crown Point T&RSMD	03, 08/0	
NH	LM	Newton Heath TMD	—	Locomotive stabling
NL	E	Neville Hill T&RSMD	08/0, 254	
OC	W	Old Oak Common TMD	08/0, 31/4, 47/4, 50	Locomotive depot
OO	W	Old Oak Common HSTD	253	HST Depot
OX	W	Oxford LIP	—	Locomotive stabling
PB	E	Peterborough Loco SD	—	Locomotive fuelling and stabling
PH	SC	Perth LIP	08/0	
PM	W	St Philips Marsh, Bristol HSTD	253	HST Depot
PO	SC	Polmadie (Glasgow) TMD	—	Locomotive repair shops
PZ	W	Penzanze Loco SD	08/0	
RG	W	Reading TMD	08/0, 97/6	
RL	E	Ripple Lane Loco SD	—	Locomotive fuelling and stabling
RR	W	Radyr HS	97/6	Locomotive stabling
RY	S	Ryde, Isle of Wight EMD	97/8	
SB	E	Shirebrook Loco SD	08/0	
SE	S	St Leonards West Marina T&RSMD	—	Locomotive repair shops
SF	E	Stratford TMD *(Sparrow)*	08/0, 31/1, 37/0, 37/5, 47/0, 47/4	
SG	S	Slade Green T&RSMD	97/8	Wheel lathe. Locomotive and repair shops
SI	LM	Soho (Birmingham) OHLD	—	Locomotive fuelling, all stock stabling
SL	S	Stewarts Lane T&RSMD	33/0, 33/2, 73/0, 73/1	Wheel lathe
SP	M	Springs Branch Wigan TMD	08/0	
SR	E	Stratford Major Depot (formerly TRS)	—	Wheel lathe. Traction repair shops
ST	W	Severn Tunnel Junction Loco SD	—	Locomotive stabling

Code	*Rgn*	*Name*	*Classes allocated*	*Notes*
SU	S	Selhurst T&RSMD	08/0, 09	Locomotive repair depot
SW	W	Swindon Loco SD	08/0	
SY	LM	Saltley (Birmingham) Loco SD	—	Locomotive stabling
TE	E	Thornaby (Tees) TMD (*Kingfisher*)	08/0, 31/1, 37/0, 37/5, 47/0, 47/3	Wheel lathe
	LM	Tibshelf HS	—	Locomotive stabling (weekdays)
TI	E	Tinsley (Sheffield) TMD	08/0, 20, 37/0, 37/5, 45/0, 45/1, 47/0, 47/3, 47/4, 56	
TJ	SC	Thornton Loco FP	—	Locomotive fuelling and stabling
TN	W	Taunton Fairwater PAD	97/6	
TO	LM	Toton TMD *(Rabbit)*	08/0, 20, 31/1, 47/0, 47/4, 56, 58	Wheel lathe. Heavy maintenance on HQ (RTC-D) main line diesel locomotives
TS	LM	Tyseley (Birmingham) TMD	08/0	Wheel lathe. Locomotive repair shops
TY	E	Tyne Yard LIP	—	Locomotive stabling
VR	LM	Aberystwyth (Vale of Rheidol line)	98	Narrow gauge steam locomotives
	M	Warrington HS		Locomotive stabling
WD	S	East Wimbledon EMUD	—	Wheel lathe
WK	LM	Workington	—	Locomotive stabling
WN	LM	Willesden TMD	08/0, 82, 83, 86/0, 86/1, 86/2, 86/3, 86/4, 87/0	Wheel lathe
WY	W	Westbury Loco SD	—	Locomotive fuelling and stabling
	E	Worksop HS	—	Locomotive stabling
YK	E	York LIP	08/0	Locomotive inspection point

(**Ss**) Stored serviceable (**Su**) Stored unserviceable

British Rail Engineering Ltd Works

Stock normally overhauled or repaired

ZC	Crewe	20, 37, 47, 81, 82, 83, 85, 86, 87	Classes 87/2 and 91 construction
ZD	Derby, Litchurch Lane	253(T), 254(T)	
ZE	Derby (Locomotive)	03, 08, 20, 25, 45, 253(P), 254(P)	
ZF	Doncaster	31, 56, 58	
ZG	Eastleigh	08, 09, 33, 73	
ZH	Glasgow	08, 20, 26, 27 (Unclassified repairs only to March 1987)	
ZN	Wolverton	Multiple-Units	Class 08 stable

Under a new BR policy announced in 1986 only major overhauls are scheduled to be carried out at BREL Works from April 1987. Heavy repairs will then be the responsibility of British Rail Maintenance Group (BRMG) workshops which will include the sites at Doncaster and Glasgow. More details will be announced in our magazines as soon as the full implications of these revised arrangements become clear.

Class 03 0-6-0DM No 03 112 stands at March (Whitemoor) cripple sidings on 19 April 1986 whilst in course of transfer from Gateshead to Colchester. *Mike Collins*

Diesel Locomotives

Class 03 0-6-0

Built: British Rail 1958-61
Engine: Gardner 4-cyl 8L3 of 204bhp (152kW)
Weight: 30 tonnes
Brake force: 13 tonnes
Maximum tractive effort: 15,300lb (68.1kN)
Transmission: Mechanical. Vulcan-Sinclair type 23 fluid coupling. Wilson-Drewry Type CA5 R7 type five-speed epicyclic gearbox. Type RF 11 spiral bevel reverse and final drive unit
Route availability: 1
Maximum speed: 28½mph
Fuel: 300gal
Train brakes: All Dual

03 059	CR	*Edward*

03 063	GD	03 158	NC
03 066	GD	03 162	BD
03 073	BD	03 170	BD
03 078	GD	03 179	CR
03 084	NC	03 197	NC
03 089	NC	03 371	GD
03 094	GD	03 397	NC
03 112	NC	03 399	CR

Allocations: **BD** 3
CR 3, **GD** 5, **NC** 6 (**17**)

Class 08/0 0-6-0

Built: British Rail 1953-62
Engine: English Electric 6-cyl 6KT of 400bhp (315kW)
Weight: 49 tonnes
Brake force: 19 tonnes
Maximum tractive effort: 35,000lb (156kN)
Power/control equipment: English Electric. Two EE 506 traction motors. Double reduction gear drive
Route availability: 5
Maximum speed: 15mph except the following which are 20mph:- 08202, 08 375/85, 08 414, 08 642/50/53/55, 08 811/30/31/33/37/92, 08 929/33
Fuel: 668gal
Train brakes: *Dual* except *Air only*: 08 388/89/90/93/97/99, 08 401/02/05/07/10/11/13/14/16-19/21/23/28/40/41/42/45/47/48/49/60/62/63/66/72/80/82-85/89/92/93/96/98/99, 08 502-07/09-17/19/21/82/86, 08 621/27/56/57/59/61/63/69/70/72/78/86-89/96/98, 08 700/03/05/07/08/13/20/26/28/29/36/70/74/76/82/85/86/89/91/93/96, 08 806/10-14/20/23-29
Vacuum only: 08 011-08 386/94/95, 08 400/06/08/20/34/36/39/44/56/58/59/61/68/75-79/87/94, 08 508/56/79, 08 606/08/26/39/60/71/84, 08 715/16/22/69/79
Special liveries:
Green: 08 011, 08 556, 08 604, 08 944
Black (LMS): 08 601
Blue (GE): 08 833
Railfreight: 08 466, 08 535, 08 765, 08 805/93

08 011	BY	*Haversham*

08 102	LN	08 297	LR
08 141	TI	08 305	HM
08 168	BG	08 308	HM
08 177	BG	08 309	KY
08 191	LE	08 331	DR
08 202	CF	08 334	TE
08 206	HM	08 335	TI
08 210	YK	08 337	DR
08 224	LN	08 361	CF
08 250	NC	08 367	LE
08 253	BG	08 375	CF
08 258	MR	08 385	DR
08 272	TI	08 386	LN
08 285	SB	08 388	IM
08 295	TE	08 389	TI
08 296	BG		

08 390	CD	*Berni*

08 393	SF	08 395	SP
08 394	LE		

08 397		FH	08 439		IM
08 399		DY	08 440		SF
08 400		LE	08 441		GD
08 401		FH	08 442		GD
08 402		KD	08 445		FH
08 405		IM	08 447		KD
08 406		MR	08 448		DY
08 407		CR	08 449		AY
08 408		CW	08 451		WN
08 410	E	SW	08 454		WN
08 411		TE	08 456		CD
08 413		SF	08 458		BY
08 414		SF	08 459		DR
08 415		AN	08 460		CR
08 416		DY	08 461		CF
08 417		SF	08 462		DY (Su LR)
08 418		MR	08 463		DY
08 419		KD	08 466	R	BS
08 420		DR	08 468		CH
08 421		HA	08 472		CD
08 423		SP	08 475		SP
08 428		DY	08 478		IM
08 434		TI	08 479		CF
08 436		BH			

08 480 E OC *Old Oak Common 1882-1982*

08 481		CF	08 487		CF
08 482		DY	08 489		CH (Su CD)
08 483	E	BR	08 492	R	TI
08 484		BY	08 493		MR
08 485		GD	08 494		WN

08 495 CA *Bury*

08 496		CA	08 499		BG
08 498		CR	08 500	R	TI

08 502 TE *Tees*

08 503		HM	08 509		BH
08 504		TE	08 510	R	TI
08 506		TE	08 511		DY
08 507		TI	08 512		GD
08 508		IM	08 514		DR

08 515		HA	08 519		TE
08 516		KY	08 521		SF
08 517		NL	08 523		OC

08 525 R YK *[Percy the Pilot]*

08 526		MR	08 530		CR
08 527		SF	08 531		SF
08 528		CA	08 532		AN
08 529		CA	08 533		WN

08 534 AN *Edge Hill*

08 535	R	TS	08 541		SF
08 536		DY	08 542		SF
08 537		IM	08 543		TI
08 538		MR	08 544		GD
08 539		MR	08 556		BY
08 540		YK	08 561		ML

08 562 DR *The Doncaster Postman*

08 565		ML	08 581	RP	ML
08 567		BG	08 582		TE
08 568	R	ML	08 583		YK
08 569	R	AN	08 584		LA
08 570		HA	08 585		CD
08 571		HA	08 586		KD
08 573		WN	08 587		GD
08 575		TE	08 588		TE
08 576		LA	08 589	R	CF
08 577	P	GD	08 590		NL
08 578		GD	08 591	P	AY
08 579		HM	08 593		SF
08 580		CA			

08 594 CA *Ely*

08 595		YK	08 599	R	CD
08 597		TO			

08 601 R TS *Sceptre*

08 603 BS

08 604 R TS *Phantom*

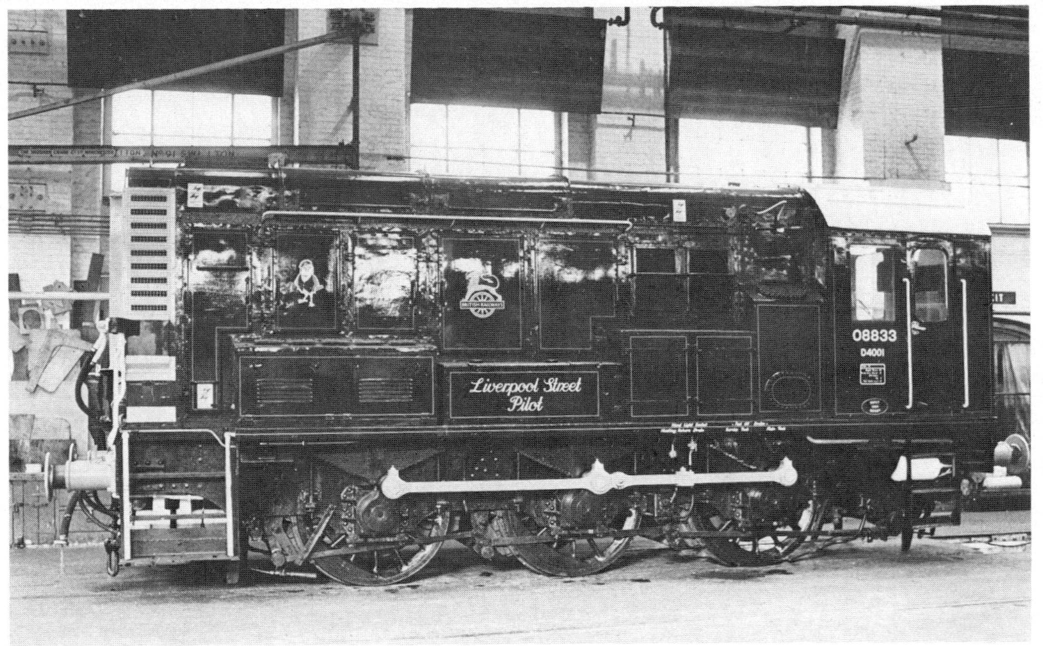

Class 08/0 0-6-0DE No 08 883 as repainted by Stratford depot. Note Stratford's Cockney Sparrow emblem, the pre-TOPS number and 'Liverpool Street Pilot' lettering. The locomotive is painted in Great Eastern blue livery. *Brian Morrison*

08 605-08 767

Number		Depot	Name
08 605	R	YK	
08 606		CW	
08 607		DR	
08 608		GD	
08 609		WN	
08 610	R	TS	
08 611		LO	
08 612		WN	
08 613		CD	
08 614	R	WN	
08 615		AN	
08 616	R	TS	*Swindon*
08 617		WN	
08 618		GD	
08 619		LO	
08 620		GM	
08 621		IS	
08 622		DY	
08 623	R	TO	
08 624		LO	
08 625		DY	
08 626		LO	
08 627		CR	
08 628		BY	
08 629		BY	*Wolverton*
08 630		GM	
08 631	R	MR	
08 632		FH	
08 633		CH	
08 634		OC	
08 635		CH	
08 637	R	CF	
08 638		CA	*Cambridge*
08 639		LE	
08 640		RG	
08 641	E	LA	*Laira*
08 642		EH	
08 643	E	BR	
08 644		PZ	
08 645	E	LA	
08 646		CF	
08 647		DR	
08 648		WN	
08 649	E	LE	
08 650		EH	
08 651	E	OC	
08 652		CF	
08 653		SU	
08 654	PT	CF	
08 655		SF	
08 656		DY	
08 657		YK	
08 658		NC	
08 659		HM	
08 660		LE	
08 661		CR	
08 662		YK	
08 663	E	LE	
08 664	R	CF	
08 665		IM	
08 666		LO	
08 667		NL	
08 668	R	CF	
08 669		AN	
08 670		WN	
08 671		GD	
08 672		BS	
08 673		LO	
08 675	R	AY	
08 676		LO	
08 677	R	CW	
08 678		TI	

Number		Depot	Name
08 680		AB	*Northern Lights*
08 682		DR	
08 683		WN	
08 685		SF	
08 686		LO	
08 687		DY (Su LR)	*Tom*
08 688		AN	
08 689		SF	
08 690		KD	
08 691		YK	
08 692		TS	
08 693		AY	
08 694		CD	
08 695		CD	
08 696		DY	
08 697		TO	
08 698		SF	
08 699		CD	
08 700		BS	
08 701		HM	
08 702		TO	
08 703		CD	
08 704		BY	
08 705		CA	
08 706		HM	
08 707		YK	
08 708		CR	
08 709		SF	
08 710		HA	
08 711		MR	
08 712		PH	
08 713		MR	
08 714		CA	
08 715		SF	
08 716		CA	
08 717		IS	
08 718		HA	
08 719		YK	
08 720	R	ML	
08 721		LO	
08 722		GD	
08 723		DR	
08 724		SF	
08 725		GM	
08 726		HA	
08 727		AY	
08 728		ML	
08 729		SB	
08 730		HA	
08 731		ML	
08 732	R	ML	
08 733	R	ML	
08 734		DR	
08 735		AY	
08 736		ML	
08 737		CD	
08 738	R	ML	
08 739		CD	
08 740		SF	
08 741		GD	
08 742		TS	
08 743		IM	
08 744		SP	
08 745		BG	
08 746		CH	
08 747		GD	
08 748		NL	
08 749		TI	
08 750		SF	
08 751		IM	
08 752		CR	
08 753		PH	
08 754		IS	
08 755		HA	
08 756		BR	
08 757		MR	
08 758		SF	
08 759		KD	
08 760		CF	
08 761		HA	
08 762		PH	
08 763		HA	
08 764		HA	
08 765	R	BS	
08 766		NL	
08 767		CR	

08 768	CW	08 778	GL
08 769	LE	08 779	CF
08 770	TE	08 780 R	LE
08 771	YK	08 781	GL
08 772	CR	08 782	KY
08 773	HM	08 783	TI
08 774	TE	08 784	CD
08 775	NC	08 785 E	CF
08 776 R	BG	08 786	TE
08 777	BG	08 787	CF

08 788 CH *Caergybi*

08 789	BY	08 798 R	LE
08 790	LO	08 799	GL
08 791	ML	08 800	BR
08 792 R	LA	08 801	BZ
08 793	ML	08 802	GD
08 794 E	NL	08 803 R	RG
08 795 R	SW	08 804 R	CF
08 796	CF	08 805 R	TS
08 797	GD		

08 806 BY *Shaw*

08 807	BY	08 811	SF
08 808	KD	08 813	SF
08 809	AN	08 814	DY
08 810	SF	08 815	SP

08 817 TE *Thornaby*

08 818 R	CF	08 826	KD
08 819 R	BR	08 827	DY
08 820	LO	08 828	SF
08 821	OC	08 829	DY
08 822	CF	08 830	EH
08 823	CD	08 831	EH
08 824	SB	08 832	BS
08 825	WN		

08 833 R SF *Liverpool Street Pilot*

08 834 E	SF	08 839	LA
08 835 E	CF	08 840	LA
08 836	GL	08 841	BS
08 837	SU	08 842	DY
08 838	AN		

08 843 CH *Holyhead*

08 844	KD	08 850	RG
08 845	EH	08 851	ED
08 846	AN	08 852	ED
08 847	EH	08 853 R	ML
08 848 T	CF	08 854	EH
08 849	SW		

08 855 AB *Hatton Castle*

08 856	CH	08 880	TI
08 857 R	TI	08 881	HA
08 858	AN	08 882	AB
08 859	CR	08 883	ML
08 865	MR	08 884	AN
08 866	DR	08 885	DR
08 867	TE	08 886	GD
08 868	NC	08 887	CW
08 869	NC	08 888 E	GD
08 870	TI	08 889	MR
08 871	BH	08 890	WN
08 872	GD	08 891	LO
08 873	SF	08 892	EH
08 874 E	NL	08 893 R	TS
08 875	NL	08 894	TO
08 876	DR	08 895 R	LE
08 877	FH	08 896	LE
08 878	TI	08 897	LE
08 879	TI	08 898	LE

08 899 DY *Percy*

08 900	BR	08 915	LO
08 901	BS	08 916	AN
08 902	AN	08 917	AN
08 903	DR	08 918	AN
08 904	WN	08 919	TI
08 905	WN	08 920	TS
08 906	TE	08 921	CD
08 907	CD	08 922	AN
08 908	LR	08 923	AN
08 909	BY	08 924	AN
08 910	KD	08 925	SP
08 911	KD	08 926	WN
08 912	KD	08 927	CH
08 913	CD	08 928	TS
08 914	LO	08 929	EH

08 930		SF	08 942		CF
08 931		GD	08 943		CW
08 932	T	CF	08 944		OC
08 933		EH	08 945		BZ
08 934		WN	08 946		RG
08 935		BR	08 947		OC
08 936		OC	08 948	R	OC
08 937		LA	08 949	R	BR
08 938	R	ML	08 950		BR
08 939		AN	08 951		BR
08 940	T	CF	08 952		ED
08 941		LA			

08 953 LA *Plymouth*

08 954		LA	08 957		SF
08 955	R	LA	08 958		SF
08 956		CR			

Allocations: **BG** 9, **BH** 3, **CA** 10, **CR** 12, **DR** 16, **FH** 5, **GD** 20, **HM** 9, **IM** 9, **KY** 3, **LN** 3, **MR** 13, **NC** 5, **NL** 8, **SB** 3, **SF** 31, **TE** 15, **TI** 19, **YK** 12
AN 20, **BS** 8, **BY** 11, **CD** 17, **CH** 9, **CW** 6, **DY** 19, **KD** 12, **LO** 14, **LR** 2, **SP** 6, **TO** 5, **TS** 11, **WN** 18
AB 3, **AY** 6, **ED** 3, **GM** 3, **HA** 13, **IS** 3, **ML** 16, **PH** 3
EH 10, **SU** 2
BR 10, **BZ** 2, **CF** 27, **GL** 4, **LA** 12, **LE** 16, **OC** 9, **RG** 4, **PZ** 1, **SW** 3 **(510+3 stored)**

Class 08/9 0-6-0

Built: British Rail 1956-59
Details as Class 08/0 except overall height reduced to 11ft 10in for operation of Cwm Mawr line (BPGV)
Maximum speed: 15mph except 08 991 which is 20mph
Train brakes: Vacuum except 08 993 which has Dual
Headlights: All fitted

08 991 (08 203)	LE	*Kidwelly*
08 992 (08 259)	LE	*Gwendraeth*
08 993 (08 592)	LE	*Ashburnham*

Allocations: **LE** 3 **(3)**

Class 09 0-6-0

Built: British Rail 1959-62
Engine: English Electric 6-cyl 6KT of 400bhp (315kW)
Weight: 49 tonnes
Brake force: 19 tonnes
Maximum tractive effort: 25,000lb (112kN)
Power/control equipment: English Electric. Two EE 506 traction motors. Double reduction gear drive
Route availability: 5
Maximum speed: 27mph
Fuel: 668gal
Train brakes: All Dual

09 001		EH	09 013		AF
09 002		SU	09 014		SU
09 003		SU	09 015		EH
09 004		SU	09 016		SU
09 005		SU	09 017	R	SU
09 006		SU	09 018		AF
09 007		SU	09 019		AF
09 008		AF	09 020		SU
09 009		SU	09 021		AF
09 010		SU	09 022		AF
09 011		AF	09 023		AF
09 012		SU	09 024		SU

09 025 R EH *Victory*

09 026 R EH

Allocations: **AF** 8, **EH** 4, **SU** 14 **(26)**

Class 20 Bo-Bo★

Built: English Electric 1957-68
Engine: English Electric 8 SVT Mk 2 of 1,000bhp (746kW)
Weight: 73 tonnes
Brake force: 35 tonnes
Maximum tractive effort: 42,000lb (187kN)
Power/control equipment: English Electric. Four EE 526/5D (20 001-049), 526/8D (20 051-20228) traction motors

Route availability: 5
Maximum speed: 75mph
Fuel: 380gal except 20 084 which has 1,040gal
Train brakes: All Dual
Guard's emergency brake valve fitted to all except 20 153/62/74
Snowplough brackets: 20 028-34/70-20 127/29-88/90-20228, 20 228
Remote control radio: 20 058/87
Transponder coding equipped: 20 001/04/06/16/20/26/41/49/52/53/65/72/73/80/81/82/99, 20 101/05/13

20 001	GMS	TO
20 002	MS	TI
20 004	MS	TO
20 005	GMS	TO
20 006	GMS	TO
20 007	GMS	TO
20 008	MS	TO
20 009		BS
20 010	M	TO
20 011	M	TI
20 013	MS	BS
20 015	M	TI
20 016	GMS	TO
20 019	S	TO
20 020	GMS	TO
20 021	S	BS
20 022	M	TI
20 023(a)	GMS	TO
20 025	M	TI
20 026	MS	TO
20 028	GS	TE
20 029	M	BS
20 030		TI
20 031	M	TI
20 032	MS	BS
20 034	S	TO
20 035		TI
20 037		BS
20 040	M	TO
20 041	MS	TO
20 042	M	BS
20 043	M	TI
20 044	M	TI
20 045	S	TO
20 046	M	TI
20 047	S	TO
20 048	M	ML
20 049	GMS	TO
20 051	GMS	TO
20 052	GMS	TO
20 053	MS	TO
20 054		TI
20 055	GMS	TO
20 056	GMS	BS
20 057	GMS	BS
20 058	GMS	TO
20 059(a)	GMS	TO
20 060	MS	BS
20 061	M	TI
20 063	M	ED
20 064		TI
20 065	MS	TO
20 066	M	TI
20 067		TO
20 068	M	TI
20 069		TI
20 070	S	TE
20 071	MS	TO
20 072	MS	TO
20 073	MS	TO
20 075	S	TO
20 076		TI
20 077	S	TO
20 078	S	TO
20 080	MS	TO
20 081	GMS	TO
20 082	MS	TO
20 083	M	TI
20 084	GMS	BS
20 085	MS	TO
20 086	M	TI
20 087	GMS	TO
20 088	M	TI
20 089	M	TI
20 090	S	TO
20 092		TI
20 093		TI
20 094	GMS	BS
20 095	M	TI
20 096	M	TI
20 097		BS
20 098	M	TI
20 099	GMS	TO
20 100	M	TI
20 101	GMS	TO
20 102	M	TI
20 103		TO
20 104	GMS	TO
20 105	GMS	TO
20 106	GMS	TO
20 107	M	TI
20 108	S	BS
20 110	M	TI
20 111	M	TI
20 112	M	TI
20 113	GMS	TO
20 114	M	ML
20 115	M	TI
20 116		TI
20 117	GS	BS
20 118	M	TI
20 119	M	TI
20 120	S	TO
20 121		TO
20 122	M	TI
20 123	M	TO
20 124	M	TO
20 126	M	TI
20 127	M	ML
20 128	GMS	TO
20 129	GS	TO
20 130	GS	TO
20 131	S	BS
20 132	S	BS
20 133	GS	BS
20 134(a)	GMS	TO
20 135	S	TO
20 136		BS
20 137	M	ED
20 138	M	ED
20 139		TI
20 140	S	TO
20 141	S	TO
20 142	GS	TO
20 143	GS	TO
20 144		TI
20 145	M	TI
20 146		TI
20 147	GS	TO
20 148		TI
20 149	S	TO
20 150		TI
20 151		TO
20 152		TI
20 153		TI
20 154	M	TO
20 155		TI
20 156	M	TI
20 157	S	TO
20 158	S	TO
20 159	S	TO
20 160	S	TO
20 161	MS	TO
20 162		TI
20 163	M	TO
20 164		TI
20 165		TI
20 166	GS	BS
20 167		TI
20 168(a)	GMS	TO
20 169	MS	TO
20 170	S	TO
20 171	M	ML
20 172(a)	GMS	TE
20 173(a)	GMS	TE
20 174		TI
20 175	MS	TI
20 176		TI
20 177	S	TO
20 178	S	TO

20 179	MS	ML	20 205	MS	ED
20 180	S	TO	20 206	S	ED
20 181	MS	ML	20 208	MS	ED
20 182		TO	20 209	GS	TO
20 183	GS	BS	20 210		BS
20 185		TO	20 211	MS	ED
20 186	GS	TO	20 212	MS	HA
20 187		TO	20 213	MS	HA
20 188	MS	TO	20 214	GS	TO
20 189	MS	ML	20 215	GS	TO
20 190	GS	TO	20 216	MS	HA
20 191	MS	ED	20 217	MS	HA
20 192	MS	ED	20 218	MS	HA
20 193	MS	ED	20 219	MS	HA
20 194(a)	GMS	TO	20 220	MS	HA
20 195	S	TO	20 221	MS	HA
20 196(a)	GMS	TO	20 222	MS	HA
20 197		BS	20 223	MS	HA
20 198	MS	ED	20 224	MS	HA
20 199	MS	ED	20 225	MS	HA
20 201	MS	ED	20 226	MS	ML
20 202	MS	ED	20 227	MS	ML
20 203	MS	ED	20 228	M	ML
20 204	MS	ED			

(a) From April to November 1986 20 023/59, 20 134/68/72/73/94/96 were numbered 20 301-08 respectively.

Notified too late for inclusion in the main body of the text are the following unofficial names: 20 028 *Bedale*; 20 172 *Redmire*; 20 173 *Wensleydale*.

Allocations: **TE** 4, **TI** 56
BS 23, **TO** 86
ED 16, **HA** 12, **ML** 10 (**207**)

Class 25/1 Bo-Bo★

Built: British Rail 1963
Engine: Sulzer 6-cyl 6LDA-28-B of 1,250bhp (933kW)
Mechanical parts: BR
Weight: 75 tonnes
Brake force: 38 tonnes
Maximum tractive effort: 45,000lb (200kN)
Power/control equipment: GEC Series 1. Four AEI 253 AY traction motors
Route availability: 5
Maximum speed: 90mph
Fuel: 500gal
Train brakes: All Dual
Snowplough brackets: 25 035/37/59
Train heat: All isolated

25 035	CD	25 058	CD
25 037	CD	25 059	CD
25 057	CD		

Allocation: **CD** 5 (**5**)

Class 25/2 Bo-Bo★

Details as Class 25/1 except:
Built: 1963-66
Power/control equipment: GEC series 2. Four AEI 253 AY traction motors
Weight: 71-76 tonnes
Train brakes: All Dual
Snowplough brackets: 25 191, 25 201
Train heat: Not equipped

25 109	CD	25 191	CD
25 173	CD	25 199	CD
25 175	CD	25 201	CD
25 176	CD	25 213	CD
25 190	CD		

Allocation: **CD** 9 (**9**)

Class 25/3 Bo-Bo★

Details as Class 25/1 except:
Built: British Rail, except 25 278/79/88 by Beyer-Peacock Ltd, 1966
Power/control equipment: GEC Series 3. Four AEI 253 AY traction motors
Weight: 71 tonnes
Train brakes: All Dual
Snowplough brackets: 25 313/23
Train heat: Not equipped

Class 20 Bo-Bo No 20 048 is seen stabled between duties at Fort William holding sidings on 26 July 1986. Fort William no longer has a resident '08' shunter and the Class 20 acts as station pilot. *Paul Biggs*

25 249	CD	25 288	CD
25 265	CD	25 313	CD
25 278	CD	25 323	CD
25 279	CD		

Allocation: **CD** 7 (**7**)

Class 25/9 Bo-Bo★

Details as Class 25/3 except:
Built: Beyer Peacock Ltd 1966, except 25901-2 British Rail 1966
Maximum speed: 60mph
Snowplough brackets: 25910/12

25 901 (25262)	KM	25 904 (25283)	KM
25 902 (25268)	KM	25 910 (25315)	KM
25 903 (25276)	KM		

25 912 (25322) KM *Tamworth Castle*

Allocation: **KM** 6 (**6**)

Class 26/0 Bo-Bo★

Built: Birmingham RC&W Ltd 1958-59
Engine: Sulzer 6-cyl 6LDA28B of 1,160bhp (865kW)
Weight: 75 tonnes (26 001-07) 79 tonnes (26 008-015)
Brake force: 35 tonnes
Maximum tractive effort: 42,000lb (187kN)
Power/control equipment: Crompton Parkinson. Four CP171A1 traction motors
Route availability: 6
Maximum speed: 75mph
Fuel: 500gal
Train brakes: All Dual
Snowplough brackets: 26 008
Train heat: Not equipped
One Man operation: All equipped
Slow Speed control: 26001-07
All refurbished

26 001	HA	26 007	HA
26 002	HA	26 008	HA
26 003	HA	26 010	HA
26 004	HA	26 011	HA
26 005	HA	26 014	HA
26 006	HA	26 015	HA

Allocation: **HA** 12 (**12**)

Class 26/1 Bo-Bo ★

Built: Birmingham RC&W Ltd, 1959
Engine: Sulzer 6-cyl 6LDA28B of 1,160bhp (865kW)
Brake force: 35 tonnes
Maximum traction effort: 42,000lb (187kN)
Power/control equipment: Crompton Parkinson. Four CP C171 D3 traction motors
Route availability: 6
Maximum speed: 75mph
Fuel: 500gal
Train brakes: All Dual
Snowplough brackets: All fitted
Train heat: Not equipped
One Man operation: All equipped
All refurbished

26 021	HA	26 035	HA
26 023	HA	26 036	HA
26 024	HA	26 037	HA
26 025	HA	26 038	HA
26 026	HA	26 039	HA
26 027	HA	26 040	HA
26 028	HA	26 041	HA
26 029	HA	26 042	HA
26 031	HA	26 043	HA
26 032	HA	26 046	HA
26 034	HA		

Allocation: **HA** 21 (**21**)

Class 27/0 Bo-Bo★

Built: Birmingham RC&W Ltd 1961-62
Engine: Sulzer 6-cyl 6LDA28-B of 1,250bhp (933kW)
Weight: 72-77 tonnes
Brake force: 35 tonnes
Maximum tractive effort: 40,000lb (178kN)
Power/control equipment: Four GEC WT459 traction motors
Route availability: 5 (27 001-056) 6 (27 059/63/66)
Maximum speed: 90mph
Fuel: 500gal except, 600gal (27 024/25/26), 685gal (27 046-56), 970gal (27 059/63/66)
Train brakes: All Dual
Snowplough brackets: All fitted
Train heat: Isolated on 27 001-08/46-56
One man operation: All equipped except 27049/51/54
All refurbished

27 001	ED	27 025	ED
27 003	ED	27 026	ED
27 005	ED	27 038	ED
27 008	ED	27 042	ED
27 024	ED		

27 046 (27 102)	ED
27 049 (27 105)	ED
27 050 (27 106)	ED
27 051 (27 107)	ED
27 052 (27 108)	ED
27 053 (27 109)	ED
27 054 (27 110)	ED
27 055 (27 111)	ED
27 056 (27 112)	ED
27 059 (27 205)	ED
27 063 (27 209)	ED
27 066 (27 212)	ED

Allocation: **ED** 21 (**21**)

Class 31/1 A1A-A1A ★

Built: Brush Traction 1959-62
Engine: English Electric 12-cyl 12CV of 1,470bhp (1,097kW)
Weight: 107-111 tonnes
Brake force: 49 tonnes
Maximum tractive effort: 42,800lb (190kN) 31 102-06/08/09/12/13, 31 250
39,500lb (160kN) all others
Power/control equipment: Brush. Four TM 73-68 traction motors
Route availability: 5
Maximum speed: 80mph (31 102/05/06/08/09/12/13, 31 250), 90mph all others
Fuel: 530gal except 31 178 which has 1,230gal capacity
Train brakes: All Dual except Vacuum only 31 271
Train heat: Isolated on 31 105/06/07/12/17/22/27/31/35/52/62/68/70/73/75/76/81/86/87/89/90/91/95/96, 31 205/06/08/12/18/19/22/23/24/25/31/32/35/42/49/50/59/63/64/68/72/86/93, 31 305/09/23/26/27 (none now equipped with operative boiler)

31 101		CW	31 125	MRP	KD
31 102	RML	MR	31 126	RML	MR
31 105	M	MR	31 127	M	MR
31 106	M	MR	31 128	RM	CW
31 107	M	IM	31 130	RL	CW
31 108	MR	MR	31 131		CW
31 109	M	MR	31 132	RPL	CW
31 110	RM	CW	31 134	MR	IM
31 112	M	IM	31 135	M	IM
31 113	RM	CW	31 138		CW
31 116	RML	CW	31 141	M	MR
31 117	M	CW	31 142	RMPL	BS
31 118	P	KD	31 143	R	BS
31 119		IM	31 144	ML	BS
31 120	RMP	KD	31 145	MR	BS
31 121	P	CW	31 146	RMPL	MR
31 122		KD	31 147	RM	MR
31 123		KD	31 149	M	IM
31 124		KD	31 152		BS

31 154	R	CW
31 155	RML	CW
31 156	RM	IM
31 158	RM	IM
31 159	MR	BS
31 160	RML	IM
31 161	MR	IM
31 162		BS
31 163	RML	IM
31 164	RMPL	MR
31 165	M	IM
31 166	RM	IM
31 167		BS
31 168	M	CW
31 170		IM
31 171	R	BS
31 173	M	MR
31 174	RM	IM
31 175	M	IM
31 176	M	IM
31 178		TE
31 180	RML	IM
31 181	M	IM
31 183	RM	MR
31 184	RML	MR
31 185	RML	IM
31 186	M	IM
31 187	M	IM
31 188	RML	IM
31 189		BS
31 190	M	IM
31 191	M	IM
31 195	M	IM
31 196	M	IM
31 198	RM	CW
31 199	RM	IM
31 200	RMP	KD
31 201	RML	IM
31 202	RM	IM
31 203	RML	BS
31 205	M	IM
31 206	M	IM
31 207	RML	IM
31 208	M	IM
31 209	R	BS
31 210	M	IM
31 212	M	SF
31 215	RML	TE
31 217	RM	CW
31 218	M	MR
31 219	M	MR
31 221	M	SF
31 222	M	CW
31 223	M	SF
31 224	M	SF
31 225	M	SF
31 226	RM	SF
31 227	M	SF
31 229	RM	MR
31 230	RML	SF
31 231	M	IM
31 232	M	IM
31 233	RML	IM
31 234	RL	KD
31 235	M	IM
31 237	RL	CW
31 238	RL	IM
31 240	RM	CW
31 242	M	IM
31 243	RM	IM
31 245	M	IM (Su SF)
31 247	RML	IM
31 248	RML	MR
31 249	M	MR
31 250	M	MR
31 252	RM	MR
31 255	RML	MR
31 257		BS
31 259	MP	KD
31 260	M	IM
31 261	RMP	MR (Su SF)
31 263	M	MR
31 264	M	MR
31 268	M	MR
31 270	RMLP	KD
31 271	MP	KD
31 272	M	MR
31 273	RMLP	IM
31 275	RML	KD
31 276	RML	TE
31 278	M	TE
31 280		BS
31 281	M	TE
31 282	M	TE
31 283	M	TE
31 284	M	TE
31 285	M	TE
31 286	M	IM
31 287		BS
31 288		BS
31 289		KD
31 290	RM	MR
31 292	M	MR
31 293		CW
31 294	RPL	BS
31 296	M	CW *Amlwch Freighter/Trên Nwyddau Amlwch*
31 299	RM	CW
31 301		TE
31 302	RM	CW
31 304	RMPL	IM
31 305		CW
31 306	RM	TE
31 308	RM	IM
31 309		CW
31 311		BS
31 312	RMP	MR
31 317	RML	CW
31 319	RMPL	TE
31 320	M	TE
31 322	M	TE
31 323	M	TE
31 324	RMPL	TE
31 326	P	CW
31 327	M	TE

Allocations: **IM** 48, **MR** 29, **SF** 8, **TE** 17, **BS** 16, **CW** 27, **KD 13** (**160+2 stored**)

Class 31/4 A1A-A1A ★

As Class 31/1 except:
Weight: 109-113 tonnes
Maximum tractive effort:39,500lb (160kN)
Route availability: 6
Maximum speed: 90mph
Train brakes: All Dual
Train heat: All electric alternator Brush BL100-30
Also isolated steam generator on 31 403/04/18
ETH index: 66
All equipped for one-man operation

31 401	RL	OC
31 402	RL	OC
31 403		BR
31 404		BR
31 405	RL	BR
31 406	R	BR
31 407	RL	MR
31 408	RL	MR
31 409	RL	MR
31 410	RL	MR
31 411	RL	MR
31 412	RL	MR
31 413	RL	MR
31 414	RL	MR
31 415	RL	MR
31 416	R	MR
31 417	R	MR
31 418		MR

31 419	R	MR	31 445	R	IM
31 420	RL	MR	31 446	RPL	IM
31 421	RL	MR	31 447	RL	IM
31 422	R	MR	31 448	RL	IM
31 423	L	BS	31 449	RL	IM
31 424	R	BS	31 450	RL	IM
31 425	R	BS	31 451	RL	IM
31 426	R	MR	31 452	RL	IM
31 427	R	MR	31 453	RL	IM
31 428	R	MR	31 454	RL	IM
31 429	R	MR	31 455	RL	IM
31 430	R	MR	31 456	RL	IM
31 431	R	MR	31 457	R	IM
31 432	R	IM	31 458	R	IM
31 433	R	IM	31 459	R	IM
31 434	R	IM	31 460	R	IM
31 435	R	IM	31 461	R	IM
31 437	R	IM	31 462	R	IM
31 438	R	IM	31 463	R	IM
31 439	R	IM	31 464	R	OC
31 440	R	IM	31 465	RP	OC
31 441	R	IM	31 466	RP	OC
31 442	R	IM	31 467	R	OC
31 443	R	IM	31 468	R	OC
31 444	R	IM			

31 469 (31 277) RL OC

Allocations: **IM** 31, **MR** 22
BS 3
BR 4, **OC** 8 (**68**)

Class 33/0 Bo-Bo ★

Built: Birmingham RC&W Ltd 1960-62
Engine: Sulzer 8-cyl 8LDA28 pressure-charged of 1,550bhp (1,156kW)
Weight: 77 tonnes
Brake force: 35 tonnes
Maximum tractive effort: 45,000lb (200kN)
Power/control equipment: Crompton Parkinson. Four CP C171 C2 traction motors
Route availability: 6
Maximum speed: 85mph
Fuel: 750gal
Train brakes: All Dual
Train heat: All electric generator Crompton Parkinson CAG 392 A1. (750V dc for heating only Mk 1, Mks 2, 2a, 2b and 2c stock.)
ETH index: 48
Snowplough brackets: All fitted
Special livery: *Green:* 33008

33 001		EH	33 004	M	EH
33 002	M	EH	33 005		EH
33 003		EH	33 006		EH

33 008 M EH *Eastleigh*

33 009	M	EH	33 017	M	EH
33 010		EH	33 018	M	EH
33 011		EH	33 019		EH
33 012	M	EH	33 020		EH
33 013		EH	33 021		EH
33 015		EH	33 022	M	EH
33 016	M	EH	33 023	M	EH

33 025 EH *Sultan*

33 026 M EH

33 027 EH *Earl Mountbatten of Burma*

33 028		EH	33 040	M	EH
33 029		EH	33 042		EH
33 030		EH	33 043		EH
33 031		EH	33 044		SL
33 032		EH	33 045		SL
33 033		EH	33 046		SL
33 034	M	EH	33 047		SL
33 035		EH	33 048		SL
33 037	M	EH	33 049		SL
33 038	M	EH	33 050		SL
33 039	M	EH	33 051		SL

33 052 M SL *Ashford*

33 053 M SL 33 055 SL

33 056 SL *The Burma Star*

33 057		SL	33 062	SL
33 058		SL	33 063	SL
33 059	M	SL	33 064	SL
33 060	M	SL	33 065	SL
33 061		SL		

Allocations: **EH** 38, **SL** 21 (**59**)

Class 33/1 Bo-Bo ★

As Class 33/0 except:
Built: 1960-1
Weight: 78 tonnes
All fitted for Push-Pull working in multiple with EMU stock, also Buckeye couplings

33 101		EH	33 111		EH
33 102		EH	33 112	M	EH
33 103	M	EH	33 113	M	EH
33 105	M	EH	33 114	M	EH
33 106		EH	33 115		EH
33 107		EH	33 116		EH
33 108	M	EH	33 117		EH
33 109		EH	33 118	M	EH
33 110		EH	33 119		EH

Allocation: **EH** 18 (**18**)

Class 33/2 Bo-Bo ★

As Class 33/0 except:
Built: 1962
Weight: 77 tonnes
Narrow body width 8ft 8in
Slow speed control: All fitted

33 201		SL	33 207	SL
33 202	M	SL	33 208	SL
33 203	M	SL	33 209	SL
33 204		SL	33 210	SL
33 205	M	SL	33 211	SL
33 206	M	SL	33 212	SL

Allocation: **SL** 12 (**12**)

Class 37/0 Co-Co★

Built: English Electric 1960-65
Engine: English Electric 12-cyl 12CSVT of 1,750bhp (1,306kW)
Weight: 102-108 tonnes
Brake force: 50 tonnes
Maximum tractive effort: 55,500lb (247kN)
Power/control equipment: English Electric. Six EE 538A traction motors
Main generator: English Electric Type 822/10G
Route availability: 5
Maximum speed: 80mph
Fuel: 1,689gal on 37 002/03/08/09/15/29/31/32/42/45/58/59/62-69/71/72/73/76/78/79/83/95/96/98, 37 100/01/06/17/19/31/39/62/64/65/67/85/93/94/97/98/99, 37 200/12/13/14/16/17/20/22-25/27-32/35/39/40/42/44/48/50/51/54/55/57/58/75-98, 37 303-08/20. All others 890gal
Train brakes: All Dual
Snowplough brackets: 37 011/12/14/21/25/27/31/33/35/40/43/51/85, 37114/20/23/35/49-58/69-72/74-37 308/10/11/14/20/21/25/26
Train Heat: Not fitted unless shown B or X

37 001	M	SF	37 014	XML	ED
37 002	M	IM	37 015	BML	GD
37 003	M	GD	37 016	M	SF
37 004	M	ED	37 018	M	IS
37 008	M	ED	37 019	M	SF
37 009	M	GD	37 021	XM	ED
37 010	M	TI	37 023	XM	TI
37 011	BML	ED	37 024	M	TI
37 012	BM	ED	37 025	XM	ED
37 013	M	TE			

37 027 XML ED *Loch Eil*

37 029	M	TE	37 038	M	SF
37 031	M	TI	37 040	M	TI
37 032	M	TE	37 041	X	SF
37 033	BML	ED	37 042	M	IM
37 035	BML	ED			

37 043 XML ED *[Loch Lomond]*

Class 31/1 A1A-A1A No 31 200 in Railfreight livery is seen approaching Toton with an ABS working from Burton-on-Trent-Toton. *C. J. Tuffs*

Number	Livery	Depot	Name
37 044	XM	SF	
37 045	M	TI	
37 046	M	TI	
37 047	XM	TI	
37 048	M	TI	
37 050	XM	IS	
37 051	XM	ED	
37 052	XM	SF	
37 053	M	SF	
37 054	XM	SF	
37 055	M	SF	
37 057	M	SF	
37 058	M	GD	
37 059	M	TE	
37 060	M	SF	
37 062	M	TE	*British Steel Corby*
37 063	M	TE	
37 065	M	TE	
37 066	M	TE	*British Steel Workington*
37 068	M	TE	
37 069	M	TE	*Thornaby TMD*
37 070	M	TE	
37 071	M	TE	*British Steel Skinningrove*
37 072	M	TE	
37 073	M	TE	
37 074	M	TE	
37 075	M	TE	
37 076	M	TE	
37 077	M	TE	*British Steel Shelton*
37 078	M	TE	*Teesside Steelmaster*
37 079	M	TE	
37 080	M	MR	
37 083	M	IM	
37 084	XM	SF	
37 085	XML	ED	
37 087	XM	SF	
37 089	XM	SF	
37 091	XM	SF	
37 092	XM	SF	
37 094	XM	SF	
37 095	M	TE	*British Steel Teesside*
37 096	M	TE	
37 097	M	MR	
37 098	M	TE	
37 100	M	TE	
37 101	M	TE	
37 102	XM	MR	
37 104	M	IM	
37 106	M	IM	
37 107	XM	MR	
37 109	XM	MR	
37 110	XM	MR	
37 113	M	MR	
37 114	BMTL	IS	*Dunrobin Castle*
37 116	XM	SF	
37 117	M	ED	
37 118	XM	SF	
37 119	M	IM	
37 120	M	TI	
37 121	M	TI	
37 123	M	TI	
37 126	M	TI	
37 127	M	SF	
37 128	M	TI	
37 129	M	TI	
37 130	M	TI	
37 131	M	TI	
37 132	M	IM	
37 133	M	ED	
37 135	M	BR	
37 138	MTL	MR	
37 139	M	MR	
37 140	M	MR	
37 141	M	SF	
37 142	M	MR	
37 144	MTL	MR	
37 146	M	ED	
37 147	M	LE	
37 149	M	LE	
37 151	M	ED	
37 153	M	IM	
37 154	M	IM	
37 158	M	MR	
37 159	M	SF	
37 160	M	SF	
37 162	M	BR	
37 164		CF	
37 165		CF	
37 166	M	SF	
37 167	M	BR	
37 168	M	SF	
37 169	M	TI	
37 170	M	TI	
37 174	M	MR	
37 175	ML	LA	
37 176	XM	TE	
37 177	X	LE	
37 178	XML	ED	
37 180	XM	LE	*Sir Dyfed/County of Dyfed*
37 182	X	BR	
37 183	XML	ED	
37 184	XML	ED	
37 185	M	ED	
37 188	BML	ED	*Jimmy Shand*
37 189	XM	BR	
37 191	XML	ED	*[International Youth Year 1985]*
37 193	M	TE	
37 194	M	TE	
37 196	M	LA	*Tre Pol and Pen*
37 197		CF	
37 198	M	TE	
37 199	M	GD	
37 200	M	TE	
37 201	M	IM	
37 202	M	IM	
37 203	M	IM	
37 204		BR	
37 207		LA	*William Cookworthy*

37 209	M	TI	37 219	MTL	MR
37 211	M	IM	37 220		CF
37 212	M	GD	37 221	M	IM
37 213		CF	37 222	M	CF
37 214	M	LE	37 223	M	CF
37 215	M	TI	37 224	M	CF
37 216	MTL	MR	37 225	M	IM
37 217	M	CF	37 226	M	TI
37 218	M	IM	37 227	M	CF

37 229 M CF *The Cardiff Rod Mill*

37 230	M	CF	37 247	BM	ED
37 232	M	BR	37 248	M	CF
37 233	M	BR	37 250	M	GD
37 235	M	LA	37 251	M	CF
37 237	M	LE	37 252	M	TI
37 238	M	IM	37 254		CF
37 239		CF	37 255	M	CF
37 240		CF	37 256		BR
37 241		TI	37 257	M	CF
37 242	M	GD	37 258	M	CF
37 244	M	CF	37 259	M	TE
37 245	M	TI			

37 260	BML	IS	*Radio Highland*
37 261	BMTL	IS	*Caithness*
37 262	BMTL	IS	*Dounreay*

37 263	XM	ED	37 293	M	CF
37 264	XML	ED	37 294	M	CF
37 275	M	CF	37 298	M	CF
37 278	M	CF	37 303	M	CF
37 280	M	CF	37 304		CF
37 284		CF	37 306	M	CF
37 285	M	CF	37 308		CF

37 310 (37 152)	M	ML	*British Steel Ravenscraig*
37 311 (37 156)	M	ML	*British Steel Hunterston*
37 312 (37 137)	M	ML	*Clyde Iron*
37 313 (37 145)	M	ML	
37 314 (37 190)	XM	ML	*Dalzell*
37 320 (37 026)	M	ML	*Shapfell*
37 321 (37 037)	XML	ML	*Gartcosh*
37 322 (37 049)	XM	ML	*Imperial*
37 323 (37 088)	XM	ML	*Clyde Steel*
37 324 (37 099)	XML	ML	*Clydebridge*
37 325 (37 108)	XML	ML	*Lanarkshire Steel*
37 326 (37 111)	XM	ML	*Glengarnock*

Allocations: **GD** 8, **IM** 17, **MR** 16, **SF** 26, **TE** 31, **TI** 24
ED 26, **ML** 12, **IS** 6
BR 89, **CF** 33, **LA** 4, **LE** 6 (**218**)

Class 37/4 Co-Co ★

As Class 37/0 except:
Converted 1985-86
Built: 1965
Weight: 107 tonnes
Traction alternator: Brush BA100SA
Maximum speed: 80mph
Fuel: 1,689gal
Train brakes: All Dual
Train heat: Brush alternator BAH 701
ETH Index: 30
Snowplough brackets: All fitted
All refurbished, equipped for one man operation, and fitted with headlights

37 401 (37 268)		ED	*Mary Queen of Scots*
37 402 (37 274)		ED	*Oor Wullie*
37 403 (37 307)		ED	*Isle of Mull*
37 404 (37 286)		ED	*Ben Cruachan*
37 405 (37 282)		ED	*Strathclyde Region*
37 406 (37 295)		ED	*The Saltire Society*
37 407 (37 305)		ED	*Loch Long*
37 408 (37 289)		ED	*Loch Rannoch*
37 409 (37 270)		ED	*Loch Awe*
37 410 (37 273)		ED	*Aluminium 100*
37 411 (37 290)		ED	*(Loch Lomond)*
37 412 (37 301)		ED	*(Loch Eil)*
37 413 (37 276)		ED	*Loch Eil Outward Bound*
37 414 (37 287)	T	IS	
37 415 (37 277)	T	IS	
37 416 (37 302)	T	IS	
37 417 (37 269)	T	IS	*Highland Region*
37 418 (37 271)	T	IS	*An Comunn Gardhealach*

Number		Depot	Name
37 419 (37 291)	T	IS	
37 420 (37 297)	T	IS	*The Scottish Hosteller*
37 421 (37 267)	T	IS	
37 422 (37 266)		ED	
37 423 (37 296)		ED	
37 424 (37 279)		ED	
37 425 (37 292)		ED	*Sir Robert McAlpine/Concrete Bob*
37 426 (37 299)		CF	*Y Lein Fach – Vale of Rheidol*
37 427 (37 288)		CF	*Bont Y Bermo*
37 428 (37 281)		CF	
37 429 (37 300)		CF	
37 430 (37 265)		CF	*Cwmbran*
37 431 (37 272)		CF	

Allocations: **ED** 17, **IS** 8
CF 6 (**31**)

Class 37/0 locomotives are being modified and renumbered between 37501 and 37906

Class 37/5 Co-Co ★

As Class 37/0 except:
Converted 1986-87
Weight: 106-107 tonnes
Traction alternator: Brush BA 100 SA (37 501+, 37 699—)
GEC (37 600+/—)
Maximum speed: 80mph
Fuel: 1,689gal
Train brakes: All Dual
Train heat: Not equipped
Snowplough brackets: All fitted
All refurbished, equipped for one-man operation, headlight fitted

Number	Depot	Number	Depot
37 501 (37 005)	CF	37 505 (37 028)	CF
37 502 (37 082)	CF	37 506 (37 007)	CF
37 503 (37 017)	CF	37 507 (37 036)	CF
37 504 (37 039)	CF	37 508 (37 090)	CF

Number	Depot
37 509 (37 093)	CF
37 510 (37 112)	CF
37 511 (37 103)	CF
37 512 (37 022)	TE
37 513 (37 056)	TE
37 514 (37 115)	TE
37 515 (37 064)	TE
37 516 (37 086)	SF
37 517 (37)	
37 518 (37)	
37 519 (37)	
37 520 (37)	
37 521 (37)	
37 522 (37)	
37 523 (37)	
37 524 (37)	
37 525 (37)	
37 526 (37)	
37 527 (37)	
37 528 (37)	
37 529 (37)	
37 530 (37)	
37 531 (37)	
37 532 (37)	
37 533 (37)	
37 534 (37)	
37 535 (37)	
37 536 (37)	
37 537 (37)	
37 538 (37)	
37 539 (37)	
37 540 (37)	
37 575 (37)	
37 576 (37)	
37 577 (37)	
37 578 (37)	
37 579 (37)	
37 580 (37)	
37 581 (37)	
37 582 (37)	
37 583 (37)	
37 584 (37)	
37 585 (37)	
37 586 (37)	
37 587 (37)	
37 588 (37)	
37 589 (37)	
37 590 (37)	
37 591 (37)	
37 592 (37)	
37 593 (37)	
37 594 (37)	
37 595 (37)	
37 596 (37)	
37 597 (37)	
37 598 (37)	
37 599 (37)	
37 600 (37)	
37 601 (37)	
37 602 (37)	
37 603 (37)	
37 604 (37)	
37 605 (37)	
37 606 (37)	
37 607 (37)	
37 608 (37)	
37 609 (37)	
37 610 (37)	
37 611 (37)	
37 612 (37)	
37 613 (37)	
37 614 (37)	
37 615 (37)	
37 616 (37)	
37 617 (37)	
37 618 (37)	
37 619 (37)	
37 620 (37)	
37 621 (37)	
37 622 (37)	
37 623 (37)	
37 624 (37)	
37 650 (37)	
37 651 (37)	
37 652 (37)	
37 653 (37)	
37 654 (37)	
37 655 (37)	
37 656 (37)	
37 657 (37)	
37 658 (37)	
37 659 (37)	
37 660 (37)	
37 661 (37)	

37 662 (37)
37 663 (37)
37 664 (37)
37 665 (37)
37 666 (37)
37 667 (37)
37 668 (37)
37 669 (37)
37 670 (37)
37 671 (37)
37 672 (37)
37 673 (37)
37 674 (37)
37 675 (37)
37 676 (37)
37 677 (37)
37 678 (37)
37 679 (37)
37 680 (37)
37 681 (37)
37 682 (37 236) TE
37 683 (37 187) TE
37 684 (37 134) TE
37 685 (37 234) TE
37 686 (37 172) TE
37 687 (37 181) TE
37 688 (37 205) TE
37 689 (37 195) TE
37 690 (37 171) TE
37 691 (37 179) TE
37 692 (37 122) TE
37 693 (37 210) TE
37 694 (37 192) CF
37 695 (37 157) CF
37 696 (37 228) CF
37 697 (37 243) CF
37 698 (37 246) CF
37 699 (37 253) CF

Allocations: **CF** 17
SF 1, **TE** 16 (**34**)

Class 37/7 Co-Co ★

As Class 37/5 except fitted with ballast weights:
Converted 1986-87
Weight: 120 tonnes
Traction alternator: 37 701+, 37 899—. GEC
37 800+/—. Brush BA 100 SA
Maximum tractive effort:
Route availability: 5
Maximum speed: 80mph
Fuel: 1,689gal
Slow speed control: All fitted
Train heat: Not equipped
All refurbished, equipped for one man operation, headlight fitted

37 701 (37 030) CF
37 702 (37 020) CF
37 703 (37 067) CF
37 704 (37 034) CF
37 705 ( )
37 706 ( )
37 707 ( )
37 708 ( )
37 709 ( )
37 710 ( )
37 711 ( )
37 712 ( )
37 713 ( )
37 714 ( )
37 788 ( )
37 789 ( )
37 790 ( )
37 791 ( )
37 792 ( )
37 793 ( )
37 794 ( )
37 795 ( )
37 796 ( )
37 797 ( )

37 800 (37 143) CF *Glo Cymru*
37 801 (37 173) CF *Aberddawan-Aberthaw*

37 802 (37 163) CF
37 803 (37 208) CF
37 804 ( )
37 805 ( )
37 806 ( )
37 807 ( )
37 808 ( )
37 809 ( )
37 810 ( )
37 811 ( )
37 812 ( )
37 813 ( )

37 884 ( )
37 885 ( )
37 886 ( )
37 887 ( )
37 888 ( )
37 889 ( )
37 890 ( )
37 891 ( )
37 892 ( )
37 893 ( )
37 894 (37 124) CF
37 895 (37 283) CF
37 896 (37 231) CF
37 897 (37 255) CF
37 898 (37 186) CF
37 899 (37 161) CF

Allocation: **CF** 16 (**16**)

Class 37/9 Co-Co ★

As Class 37/7 except:
Converted 1986
Engine: 37 901-04 Mirrlees MB275T, 1,800bhp (1,343kN). 37 905/06 GEC Ruston RK270T, 1,800bhp (1,343kN)
Weight: 120 tonnes
Brake force:
Traction Alternator: Brush BA 100 SA (37901-04); GEC (37905/06)
Maximum tractive effort:
Route availability: 7
Maximum speed: 80mph
Fuel: 1,689gal

37 901 (37 150)	CF	*Mirrlees Pioneer*
37 902 (37 148)	CF	
37 903 (37 249)	CF	
37 904 (37 125)	CF	
37 905 (37 136)	CF	
37 906 (37 206)	CF	

Allocation: **CF** 6 (**6**)

Class 40 1 Co-Co 1★

Built: English Electric 1958
Engine: English Electric 16-cyl 16SVT Mk 2 of 2,000bhp (1,492kW)
Weight: 136 tonnes
Brake force: 51 tonnes
Maximum tractive effort: 52,000lb (231kN)
Power/control equipment: English Electric. Six EE 526/5D traction motors
Route availability: 6
Maximum speed: 90mph
Train brakes: Dual
Fuel: 710gal
Train heat: Stone Vapor 4625 steam generator isolated
Special livery: Green
This was the first locomotive of this class and has been retained by British Rail for enthusiast specials. For this reason it also carries its original number D200

40 122	KD

Allocation: **KD** 1 (**1**)

Class 45/0 1Co-Co1 ★

Built: British Rail 1960-62
Engine: Sulzer 12-cyl 12LDA28-B of 2,500bhp (1,865kW)
Weight: 138 tonnes
Brake force: 63 tonnes
Maximum tractive effort: 55,000lb (245kW)
Power/control equipment: Crompton Parkinson. Six CP C172 A1 traction motors
Route availability: 7
Maximum speed: 90mph
Train brakes: All Dual
Fuel: 790gal
Train heat: All fitted with isolated boiler

45 007	TI	45 013	TI
45 012	TI		

45 022	TI	*[Lytham St Annes]*

45 029	TI	45 034	TI
45 033	TI	45 037	TI

45 040	TI	*[The King's Shropshire Light Infantry]*
45 041	TI	*[Royal Tank Regiment]*
45 044	TI	*[Royal Inniskilling Fusilier]*
45 046	TI	*[Royal Fusilier]*
45 049	TI	*[The Staffordshire Regiment (The Prince of Wales's)]*

45 051	TI	45 062	TI
45 052	TI	45 066	TI
45 058	TI	45 070	TI

Allocation: **TI** 19 (**19**)

On 18 May 1986 Severn Tunnel Junction depot held a 'low key' open day as part of the Severn Tunnel Celebrations. Seen here are Nos 37 229 *The Cardiff Rod Mill*, 08 896, 47 337 *Herbert Morris*, 50 007 *Sir Edward Elgar*. *Barry Nicolle*

Class 45/1 1Co-Co1 ★

As Class 45/0 except:
Weight: 135 tonnes
Route availability: 6
Train heat: Electric alternator Brush BL 100-30 Mk II
ETH Index: 66
All headlight fitted

45 103 TI

45 104 TI *[The Royal Warwickshire Fusiliers]*

45 105 TI
45 106 TI
45 107 TI
45 108 TI
45 110 TI

45 111 TI *[Grenadier Guardsman]*
45 112 TI *[The Royal Army Ordnance Corps]*

45 113 TI
45 114 TI
45 115 TI

45 118 TI *[The Royal Artilleryman]*

45 119 TI
45 120 TI
45 121 TI
45 122 TI
45 124 TI
45 125 TI
45 126 TI
45 127 TI
45 128 TI
45 129 TI
45 130 TI
45 132 TI
45 133 TI
45 134 TI

45 135 TI *[3rd Carabinier]*

45 136 TI

45 137 TI *[The Bedfordshire and Hertfordshire Regiment (TA)]*

45 139 TI
45 140 TI
45 141 TI
45 142 TI

45 143 TI *[5th Royal Inniskilling Dragoon Guards 1685-1985]*
45 144 TI *[Royal Signals]*

45 145 TI
45 146 TI
45 148 TI
45 149 TI
45 150 TI

Allocations **TI** 41 (**41**)

Class 47/0 Co-Co

Built: BR and Brush Traction 1962-67
Engine: Sulzer 12-cyl 12LDA28-C of 2,580bhp (1,925kW)
Weight: 111-121 tonnes
Brake force: 60 tonnes
Maximum tractive effort: 62,000lb (267kN)
Power/control equipment: Brush. Six TM 64-68 Mk 1 (47 002-016/096-47 124). Six TM64-68 Mk 1A (remainder)
Route availability: 6
Maximum speed: 95mph
Train brakes: All Dual
Fuel: 720gal
Train heat: See C, D, X
All refurbished, second refurbishment marked 'R'.
One Man Operation equipped: All except 47214
Headlight fitted: All except 47008/11, 47196
Special livery:
Brunswick green: 47079

47 002 BS
47 003 XP ED
47 004 DP ED
47 005 SF
47 006 XP ED

47 007 SF *Stratford*

47 008 X SF
47 009 X SF
47 010 GD
47 011 X BS
47 012 X ED
47 013 X GD
47 014 R CF
47 015 X BS
47 016 R GD
47 017 DP ED
47 018 P ED
47 019 BS
47 033 BR
47 049 C ED
47 050 BS
47 051 BS
47 052 SF
47 053 XP ED
47 054 X SF
47 060 X BS
47 063 BR

47 079 X BR *G. J. Churchward*
47 085 X BR *Mammoth*
47 089 BR *Amazon*

BR's eldest workable locomotive is Bletchley TMD's well kept Class 08 0-6-0DE No 08 011 *Haversham*, pictured here in Bletchley station on pilot duties on 17 October 1986. The locomotive is in green livery. *Barry Smith*

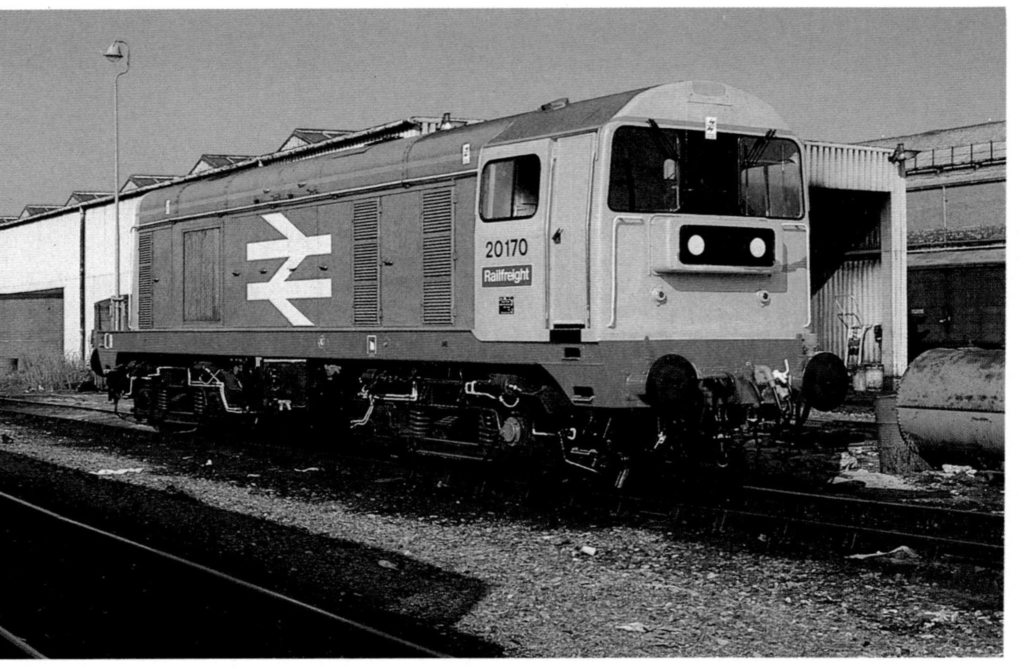

Fresh from the paint shop Class 20 Bo-Bo No 20 170 is seen stabled at Derby Holding Sidings on 17 October 1986. Painted in Railfreight livery this locomotive was the last to be dual braked. *Mark Scott*

A line-up of Class 26 motive power is seen here on 11 May 1986. Locomotive Nos 26 031 and 26 008 are in Railfreight livery whilst No 26 004 is in blue. *T. W. J. Murray*

Class 33/0 Bo-Bo No 33 008 *Eastleigh* freshly outshopped by depot volunteers on 11 October 1986 in 1964 style livery. The work was carried out during the staff's own time, with the crests being donated by the Mid Hants Railway. *David Warwick*

Class 45/0 1Co-Co1 No 45 041 heads towards Salisbury with the 08.30 ABS Severn Tunnel Junction-Eastleigh seen passing Sherrington on 29 August 1985. The locomotive is minus its *Royal Tank Regiment* nameplates. *Peter Durham*

Class 37/4 Co-Co No 37 401 *Mary Queen of Scots* shunts the empty stock at Fort William from the 05.05 ex-Glasgow, seen on 30 June 1986. *Bill Sharman*

Class 47/4 Co-Co No 47 515 *Night Mail* is seen here stabled at Preston on 12 October 1986. The locomotive is in InterCity livery. *M. Hilbert*

Sporting Network SouthEast livery Class 50 Co-Co No 50 026 *Indomitable* is seen at Yeovil Junction in October 1986. *Andrew Fox*

Standing outside BREL Doncaster on 4 May 1986 was Railfreight liveried Class 56 Co-Co No 56 007.
Colin Marsden

Privately-owned by Foster Yeoman and classified by BR as Class 59, No 59 001 *Yeoman Endeavour* passes Clink Road Junction with the 17.05 Merehead-Brentford stone train on 8 August 1986. A bell can be seen on the front of the cab. *Peter Medley*

Class 73/1 Bo-Bo No 73 123 *Gatwick Express* seen at Waterloo on 3 May 1986. *Andrew Fox*

Class 87/0 Bo-Bo No 87 012 formerly *Coeur de Lion* hauls Class 86/2 No 86 216 *Meteor* with an up Freightliner near Bugbrooke, Northampton on 12 September 1985. *John Oxley*

The 05.07 Penzance-Paddington, the 'Golden Hind' is seen passing Clink Road Junction, Frome, formed by InterCity 125 unit No 253 033 on 11 April 1986.
Peter Robinson

With locomotive and train in InterCity livery Class 86/2 Bo-Bo No 86 248 *Sir Clwyd/County of Clwyd* powers its way out of Crewe on 28 May 1986 with the 13.45 Dover Western Docks-Liverpool service. *Chris Morrison*

Preserved Class 42 B-B No D821 *Greyhound* powers the 14.55 Grosmont-Pickering into Levisham on the North Yorkshire Moors Railway, 28 April 1984. *Steve Dudman*

With a loaded MGR for Didcot power station Class 58 Co-Co No 58 038 awaits clearance at Foxhall Junction on 4 September 1986. *P. D. Quine*

47 093		BR	47 106	X	BS
47 094		BR	47 107		BS
47 095		BR	47 108	X	SF
47 096	X	SF	47 109	D	ED
47 097		CF	47 110		KD
47 098		BS	47 112		CF
47 099		CF	47 113	X	BS
47 100		CD	47 114	X	SF
47 101	X	SF	47 115	X	KD
47 102	X	CD	47 116	X	SF
47 103	X	CD	47 117	DP	ED
47 104	X	BS	47 118	XP	ED
47 105	X	SF	47 119		KD

47 120 D ED *RAF Kinloss*

47 121	X	SF	47 192	XS	CD
47 122		CD	47 193	S	CD
47 123	X	SF	47 194	XS	CD
47 124	X	SF	47 195	XS	CD
47 125		BR	47 196	XS	CD
47 130	X	BR	47 197	XS	CD
47 131		BR	47 198	S	CD
47 137	X	KD	47 199	XS	CD
47 140	X	BR	47 200	XS	KD
47 142		BR	47 201	XS	KD
47 143		BR	47 202	S	BR
47 144	X	BR	47 203	XS	KD
47 145	X	BR	47 204	S	KD
47 146	X	BR	47 205	XS	KD
47 147		BR	47 206	CP	ED
47 148	X	BR	47 207	X	CF
47 150	X	KD	47 209	C	ED
47 152	D	ED	47 210	XP	ED
47 156	X	BR	47 211		CF
47 157	X	BR	47 212		IM
47 159	X	BR	47 213	S	BR
47 162	X	BR	47 214	X	KD
47 186	S	CF	47 215	S	BR
47 187	XS	CD	47 217	X	TI
47 188	S	CD	47 218		CD
47 189	XS	CD	47 219	X	TI
47 190	S	CD	47 220	S	BR
47 191	XS	CD	47 221		IM

47 222 IM *Appleby Frodingham*

47 223	X	IM	47 237	S	CF
47 224		IM	47 238	S	CF
47 225	S	CF	47 241	S	CF
47 226	S	CF	47 245		BR
47 227	X	CD	47 249		BR
47 228	X	CD	47 256		BR
47 229	S	CD	47 258		BR
47 230	S	CF	47 270		GD
47 231	S	CF	47 276		KD
47 233	S	CF	47 277		SF
47 234	S	CF	47 278		SF
47 235	S	CF	47 279	XS	BR
47 236	S	CF			

47 280 CD *Pedigree*

47 281		CD	47 291		SF
47 283	S	BR	47 292		SF
47 284	S	BR	47 293		BR
47 285	S	BR	47 294		IM
47 286	S	BR	47 295		IM
47 287		SF	47 296		IM
47 288		SF	47 297	S	BR
47 289		SF	47 298	X	BS
47 290	X	BS	47 299		IM

Allocations: **GD** 4, **IM** 9, **SF** 22, **TI** 2
BS 14, **CD** 23, **KD** 12
ED 15
BR 38, **CF** 18 (**157**)

Class 47/3 Co-Co

As Class 47/0 except:
Built: 1964-65
Weight: 114 tonnes
Power/control equipment: Brush Six TM64-68 Mk 1A traction motors
Train Heat: Not equipped
Slow speed control fitted: 47301-10/12/14-81
All refurbished
One Man operation: All equipped except: 47358
Headlights: All fitted except: 47328/39/67

47 301	TE	47 319	TE
47 302	TE	47 320	CD
47 303	TE	47 321	CD
47 304	TE	47 322	CD
47 305	TE	47 323	CD
47 306	KD	47 324	CD
47 307	TE	47 325	CD
47 308	TE	47 326	CD
47 309	KD	47 327	BR
47 310	IM	47 328	CD
47 311	IM	47 329	BS
47 312	IM	47 330	CD
47 313	IM	47 331	CD
47 314	IM	47 332	CD
47 315	CD	47 333	CD
47 316	TI	47 334	CD
47 317	CD	47 335	CD
47 318	CD	47 336	IM

47 337 BS *Herbert Austin*

47 338	BS	47 350	CD
47 339	BS	47 351	CD
47 340	CD	47 352	CD
47 341	CD	47 353	CD
47 342	CD	47 354	CD
47 343	CD	47 355	CD
47 344	CD	47 356	CD
47 345	CD	47 357	CD
47 346	TE	47 358	CD
47 347	CD	47 359	CD
47 348	CD	47 360	TE
47 349	CD		

47 361 TE *Wilton Endeavour*

47 362 TE

47 363 TE *Billingham Enterprise*

47 364 CD

47 365 CD *Diamond Jubilee*
47 366 CD *The Institution of Civil Engineers*

47 367	CD	47 369	CD
47 368	CF	47 370	TI
47 371	TI	47 373	TI
47 372	TI		

47 374 SF *Petrolea*

47 375	TI	47 377	CD
47 376	CD	47 378	CD

47 379 IM *Total Energy*

47 380	IM	47 381	CD

Allocations: **IM** 8, **TE** 13, **TI** 5
BS 4, **CD** 45, **KD** 2
BR 1, **CF** 1 (**81**)

Class 47/4 Co-Co

As Class 47/0 except:
Weight: 120-125 tonnes
Maximum tractive effort: 55,000lb (245kN) 47 401-20; 62,000lb (275kN) remainder
Power/control equipment: Brush Six traction motors TM64-68 Mk 1; 47 401-34/85-88 others type TM64-68A
Fuel: 1,295gal; 47 551/52, 47 650-65; all others 720gal
Train heat: Electric generator Brush TG160-16 (47 401-20 only) or electric alternator Brush BL 100-30 plus steam generator where shown (D operational, X isolated)
All refurbished.
Headlight: All fitted except: 47 490, 475 34/36
Special liveries:
InterCity: 47 406 47 509/15/49, 47611/12/13
InterCity (ScotRail logo): 47 430/69/92, 47 541, 47 637/42/43
ScotRail: 47 461
Brunswick green: 47 484, 47 500, 47 628
Network SouthEast: 47 570/76/81/82/83/85

47 401	M	GD	*North Eastern*
47 402	XM	GD	*Gateshead*
47 404	XM	GD	*Hadrian*
47 406	XM	GD	*Rail Riders*
47 407	XM	GD	*Aycliffe*

47 410	XM	GD	47 417	XM	GD
47 411	M	GD	47 418	XM	GD
47 412	XM	GD	47 419	XM	GD
47 413	M	GD	47 420	XM	GD
47 415	XM	GD			

47 421	XM	GD	*The Brontës of Haworth*

47 422	M	GD	47 433	M	BS
47 423	XM	GD	47 434	M	BS
47 424	M	GD	47 435	XM	BS
47 425	XM	TI	47 436	M	BS
47 426	M	TI	47 437		CD
47 427	M	TI	47 438	M	TI
47 428	M	TI	47 439	M	TI
47 429	XM	IS	47 440		BS
47 430	M	IS	47 441		BS
47 431	M	BS	47 442	M	BS
47 432		BS	47 443	M	CD

47 444	M	CD	*University of Nottingham*

47 445		CD	47 451		CD
47 446		CD	47 452		CD
47 447	M	CD	47 453		CD
47 448	M	IS	47 454	M	CD
47 449	M	CD	47 455		CD
47 450	M	BS	47 456		CD

47 457	M	GD	*Ben Line*

47 458	M	GD	47 460	DMP	IS
47 459	M	CD			

47 461	MP	IS	*Charles Rennie Mackintosh*

47 462	M	ED	47 466	M	GD
47 463	M	CD	47 467	MP	IS
47 465	M	CD	47 468		CD

47 469	MP	ED	*Glasgow Chamber of Commerce*
47 470	MP	ED	*University of Edinburgh*
47 471	M	KD	*Norman Tunna GC*

47 472	M	BS	47 474	M	KD
47 473	M	BS	47 475	M	KD

47 476	M	GD	47 478	M	KD
47 477	M	GD	47 479		KD

47 480		KD	*Robin Hood*

47 481		KD	47 483	M	KD
47 482	M	GD			

47 484	M	OC	*Isambard Kingdom Brunel*

47 485	M	CD	47 488		CD
47 486	M	BS	47 489	M	CD
47 487	M	SF	47 490		CD

47 491	M	CD	*Horwich Enterprise*
47 492	MP	IS	*The Enterprising Scot*

47 497	M	GD

47 500	M	OC	*Great Western*

47 501	M	OC	47 503	M	KD

47 508	M	OC	*SS Great Britain*

47 509	M	OC	*Albion*

47 512		GD

47 513	M	OC	*Severn*
47 515	M	OC	*Night Mail*
47 517	M	IS	*Andrew Carnegie*

47 518	M	BS	47 522	M	GD
47 519	M	IS	47 523	XM	GD
47 520	XM	GD	47 524	XM	GD
47 521	XM	GD	47 525	XM	GD

47 526	M	GD	*Northumbria*

47 527	XM	GD	47 531		CD
47 528	XM	GD	47 532		CD
47 529		CD	47 533	M	CD
47 530	M	CD	47 534		BS

47 535	M	BS	*University of Leicester*

Number		Depot	Name
47 536	M	CD	
47 537	M	BS	*Sir Gwynedd-County of Gwynedd*
47 538		KD	*[Python]*
47 539	M	CD	*Rochdale Pioneers*
47 540	M	CD	
47 541	XMP	IS	*The Queen Mother*
47 542	XM	GD	
47 543	M	CD	
47 544	XM	GD	
47 545	M	CD	
47 546	MP	IS	*Aviemore Centre*
47 547		CD	
47 549	M	OC	*Royal Mail*
47 550	MP	IS	*University of Dundee*
47 551	M	GD	
47 552	M	GD	
47 553	M	KD	
47 555		CD	*The Commonwealth Spirit*
47 556	M	CF	
47 557	M	CF	
47 558	M	CF	*Mayflower*
47 559	M	CF	*Sir Joshua Reynolds*
47 560	M	CF	*Tamar*
47 561	M	CD	
47 562	M	ED	*Sir William Burrell*
47 563	M	ED	
47 564		CF	
47 565	M	CF	
47 566	M	GD	
47 567	M	CF	*Red Star*
47 568	M	GD	
47 569	M	GD	
47 570	M	SF	
47 571	M	KD	
47 572	M	SF	*Ely Cathedral*
47 573	M	SF	*The London Standard*
47 574	M	SF	*Lloyds List*
47 575	M	CF	*City of Hereford*
47 576	M	SF	
47 577	M	SF	*Benjamin Gimbert GC*
47 578	M	ED	*Royal Society of Edinburgh*
47 579	M	SF	*James Nightall GC*
47 580	M	SF	*County of Essex*
47 581	M	SF	*Great Eastern*
47 582	M	SF	*County of Norfolk*
47 583	M	SF	*County of Hertfordshire*
47 584	M	SF	*County of Suffolk*
47 585	M	SF	*County of Cambridgeshire*
47 586	M	IS	
47 587	M	GD	
47 588		BS	
47 589	M	CF	
47 590	M	BS	*Thomas Telford*
47 591	M	SF	
47 592	M	CF	*County of Avon*
47 593	M	ED	*Galloway Princess*
47 594	M	CF	
47 595	MP	ED	*Confederation of British Industry*
47 596	M	SF	*Aldeburgh Festival*
47 597	M	CF	
47 598		BS	
47 599	M	BS	
47 600	M	CF	*Dewi Sant — Saint David*
47 602	M	CF	*Glorious Devon*
47 603	M	CF	*County of Somerset*
47 604	MP	IS	
47 605	M	SF	
47 606	M	CF	*Odin*
47 607	M	CF	*Royal Worcester*
47 608	M	CD	

Class 47/3 No 47 361 *Wilton Endeavour* seen at Chester about to return to Edinburgh a Scotrail excursion on 22 March 1986. Note Thornaby depot's kingfisher motif. *Ronnie McAdam*

47 609	M	OC	*Fire Fly*
47 610	M	BS	
47 611	M	OC	*Thames*
47 612	M	OC	*Titan*
47 613		OC	*North Star*
47 614	M	IS	
47 615	M	CF	*Castell Caeffilli — Caerphilly Castle*
47 616	M	CF	*Y Ddraig Goch — The Red Dragon*
47 617	MP	ED	*University of Stirling*
47 618	M	OC	*Fair Rosamund*
47 619	M	CD	
47 620		OC	*Windsor Castle*
47 621	M	OC	*Royal County of Berkshire*
47 622	M	CF	
47 623	M	OC	*Vulcan*
47 624	M	CF	*Cyclops*
47 625	M	CF	*City of Truro*
47 626	M	OC	*Atlas*
47 627	M	OC	*City of Oxford*
47 628	M	OC	*Sir Daniel Gooch*

47 629 (47 266)	M	CD	47 632 (47 068)	M	BS
47 630 (47 041)	MP	IS	47 633 (47 083)	MP	IS
47 631 (47 059)	M	BS			

47 634 (47 158)	M	SF	*Henry Ford*
47 635 (47 029)	MP	ED	
47 636 (47 243)	MP	ED	*Sir John de Graeme*
47 637 (47 274)	M	IS	
47 638 (47 069)	M	BS	*County of Kent*
47 639 (47 064)	M	BS	*Industry Year 1986*
47 640 (47 244)	M	ED	*University of Strathclyde*
47 641 (47 086)	M	ED	*Fife Region*
47 642 (47 040)	M	IS	*Strathisla*
47 643 (47 269)	MP	IS	
47 644 (47 246)	MP	ED	*The Permanent Way Institution*
47 645 (47 075)	M	BS	*Robert F. Fairlie*
47 646 (47 074)	M	BS	
47 647 (47 091)	M	KD	*Thor*

47 648 (47 151)	M	KD	47 651 (47 254)	M	GD
47 649 (47 061)	M	SF	47 652 (47 055)	M	GD
47 650 (47 257)	M	GD	47 653 (47 088)	M	GD

47 654 (47 056)	M	GD	*Finsbury Park*

47 655 (47 247)	M	GD	47 661 (47 066)	M	GD
47 656 (47 128)	M	GD	47 662 (47 032)	M	GD
47 657 (47 239)	M	GD	47 663 (47 240)	M	GD
47 658 (47 129)	M	GD	47 664 (47 135)	M	GD
47 659 (47 242)	M	GD	47 665 (47 232)	M	GD
47 660 (47 155)	M	GD			

Allocations: **GD** 59, **SF** 19, **TI** 6
CD 38, **BS** 28, **KD** 14
ED 14, **IS** 20
CF 23, **OC** 19 (**240**)

Class 47/7 Co-Co

As Class 47/4 except:
Built: 1966/67 BR and Brush Traction
Modified to this specification from 1979
Weight: 119 tonnes
Maximum speed: 100mph
Fuel: 1,295gal
Train heat: Electric Alternator, Brush BL 100-30
All refurbished and equipped push-pull operation and headlights, one man operation
Special livery: *ScotRail*

47 701	HA	*Saint Andrew*
47 702	HA	*Saint Cuthbert*
47 703	HA	*Saint Mungo*
47 704	HA	*Dunedin*
47 705	HA	*Lothian*

47 706	HA	*[Waverley]*
47 707	HA	*Holyrood*
47 708	HA	*Waverley*
47 709	HA	*The Lord Provost*
47 710	HA	*Sir Walter Scott*
47 711	HA	*Greyfriars Bobby*
47 712	HA	*Lady Diana Spencer*
47 713	HA	*Tayside Region*
47 714	HA	*Grampian Region*
47 715	HA	*Haymarket*
47 716	HA	*The Duke of Edinburgh's Award*

Allocation: **HA** 16 (**16**)

Class 47/9 Co-Co

Built: BR 1964. Modified to this specification in 1979
Engine: Ruston-Paxman 12RK3CT 12cyl of 3,250hp (2,460kw)
Weight: 114 tonnes
Brake force: 60 tonnes
Maximum tractive effort: 57,325lb (516kN)
Power/control equipment: Brush Six TM64-68 Mk 1A traction motors
Route availability: 6
Train brakes: Air only
Fuel: 1,010gal
Train heat: Not fitted
Equipped for slow speed control, and one man operation

47 901	BR

Allocation: **BR** 1 (**1**)

Class 50 Co-Co ■

Built: English Electric 1967-68
Engine: English Electric 16-cyl 16CSVT of 2,700bhp (2,014kW)
Weight: 117 tonnes
Brake force: 59 tonnes
Maximum tractive effort: 48,500lb (216kN)
Power/control equipment: English Electric. Six 538/5A traction motors
Route availability: 6
Maximum speed: 100mph
Train brakes: All Dual
Fuel: 1,055gal
Train heat: Electric generator, English Electric EE915/1B
ETH index: 61
One man operation: All fitted
All refurbished and fitted with headlights
Special liveries:
Brunswick green: 50 007
Network SouthEast: 50002/17/18/19/23/26/32/34/35/37/44

50 001	LA	*Dreadnought*
50 002	LA	*Superb*
50 003	LA	*Temeraire*
50 004	LA	*St Vincent*
50 005	LA	*Collingwood*
50 006	LA	*Neptune*
50 007	LA	*Sir Edward Elgar*
50 008	LA	*Thunderer*
50 009	LA	*Conqueror*
50 010	LA	*Monarch*
50 011	LA	*Centurion*
50 012	LA	*Benbow*
50 013	LA	*Agincourt*
50 014	LA	*Warspite*
50 015	LA	*Valiant*
50 016	LA	*Barham*
50 017	LA	*Royal Oak*
50 018	LA	*Resolution*
50 019	LA	*Ramillies*
50 020	LA	*Revenge*
50 021	OC	*Rodney*
50 022	OC	*Anson*
50 023	OC	*Howe*
50 024	OC	*Vanguard*
50 025	OC	*Invincible*
50 026	OC	*Indomitable*
50 027	LA	*Lion*
50 028	LA	*Tiger*
50 029	LA	*Renown*
50 030	OC	*Repulse*

50 031	OC	*Hood*
50 032	OC	*Courageous*
50 033	OC	*Glorious*
50 034	OC	*Furious*
50 035	OC	*Ark Royal*
50 036	OC	*Victorious*
50 037	OC	*Illustrious*
50 038	OC	*Formidable*
50 039	OC	*Implacable*
50 040	OC	*Leviathan*
50 041	LA	*Bulwark*
50 042	LA	*Triumph*
50 043	LA	*Eagle*
50 044	LA	*Exeter*
50 045	LA	*Achilles*
50 046	LA	*Ajax*
50 047	LA	*Swiftsure*
50 048	LA	*Dauntless*
50 049	LA	*Defiance*
50 050	LA	*Fearless*

Allocations: **LA** 33, **OC** 17 **(50)**

Class 50/1 Co-Co ■

A modified Class 50 locomotive using the bogies and traction motors of a refurbished Class 37 locomotive and restricted to 80mph has been authorised as an experiment for the Railfreight Sector. Further details to be announced.

Class 56 Co-Co ♦

Built: Electroputere (Romania) 56 001-30 and BREL 1977-84
Engine: GEC Ruston-Paxman 16-cyl 16RK3CT of 3,250bhp (2,460kW)
Weight: 126 tonnes
Brake force: 60 tonnes
Maximum tractive effort: 49,456lb (270kN)
Power/control equipment: Brush. Six TM 73-62 traction motors
Route availability: 7
Maximum speed: 80mph
Train brakes: All Air
Fuel: 1,150gal
Train heat: Not equipped

All equipped slow-speed control, one man operation and headlights. 56 073/74 fitted for remote control 56 042 fitted with experimental CP1 bogies

56 001	BR	56 016	TO
56 002	TO	56 017	TO
56 003	TO	56 018	TO
56 004	TO	56 019	TO
56 005	TO	56 020	TO
56 006	TO	56 021	TO
56 007	TO	56 022	TO
56 008	TO	56 023	TO
56 009	TO	56 024	TO
56 010	TO	56 025	TO
56 011	TO	56 026	TO
56 012	TO	56 027	TO
56 013	TO	56 028	TO
56 014	TO	56 029	TO
56 015	TO	56 030	TO

56 031	BR	*Merehead*
56 032	CF	*Sir De Morgannwg/ County of South Glamorgan*
56 033	BR	
56 034	BR	*Castell Ogwr/Ogmore Castle*
56 035	CF	*Taff Merthyr*
56 036	BR	
56 037	CF	*Richard Trevithick*
56 038	CF	*Western Mail*
56 039	BR	
56 040	CF	*Oystermouth*

56 041	CF	56 047	TO
56 042	TO	56 048	BR
56 043	BR	56 049	BR
56 044	TO	56 050	CF
56 045	TO	56 051	BR
56 046	TO	56 052	CF

56 053	CF	*County of Mid Glamoragn — Sir Morgannwg Ganol*

56 054	TO	56 059	TO
56 055	BR	56 060	TO
56 056	BR	56 061	TO
56 057	BR	56 062	TO
56 058	TO		

56 063	TO	*Bardon Hill*

56 064	TO	56 069	TO
56 065	TO	56 070	TO
56 066	TO	56 071	TO
56 067	TO	56 072	TO
56 068	TO	56 073	TO

56 074	TO	*Kellingley Colliery*
56 075	TO	*West Yorkshire Enterprise*

56 076	TO	56 100	TI
56 077	TO	56 101	TI
56 078	TO	56 102	TI
56 079	TO	56 103	TI
56 080	TO	56 104	TI
56 081	TO	56 105	TI
56 082	TO	56 106	TI
56 083	TO	56 107	TI
56 084	TO	56 108	TI
56 085	TO	56 109	TI
56 086	TO	56 110	TI
56 087	TO	56 111	TI
56 088	TO	56 112	TI
56 089	TI	56 113	GD
56 090	TI	56 114	GD
56 091	TI	56 115	GD
56 092	TI	56 116	GD
56 093	TI	56 117	GD
56 094	TI	56 118	GD
56 095	TI	56 119	GD
56 096	TI	56 120	GD
56 097	TI	56 121	GD
56 098	TI	56 122	GD
56 099	TI	56 123	GD

56 124	GD	*Blue Circle Cement*

56 125	GD	56 129	GD
56 126	GD	56 130	GD
56 127	GD	56 131	GD
56 128	GD		

56 132	GD	*Fina Energy*
56 133	GD	*Crewe Locomotive Works*
56 134	GD	*Blyth Power*
56 135	GD	*Port of Tyne Authority*

Allocations: **GD** 23, **TI** 24, **TO** 66
BR 13, **CF** 9 (**135**)

Class 58 Co-Co ♦

Built: BREL 1983-86
Engine: GEC-Ruston-Paxman 12RK3ACT of 3,300bhp (2,460kW)
Weight: 130 tonnes
Brake force: 60 tonnes
Maximum tractive effort: 60,750lb
Power/control equipment: Brush. Six TM73-62 traction motors
Route availability: 7
Maximum speed: 80mph
Train brakes: Air
Fuel: 927gal
Train heat: Not equipped
All equipped slow speed control, one man operation, snowplough brackets and headlights

58 001	TO	58 011	TO
58 002	TO	58 012	TO
58 003	TO	58 013	TO
58 004	TO	58 014	TO
58 005	TO	58 015	TO
58 006	TO	58 016	TO
58 007	TO	58 017	TO
58 008	TO	58 018	TO
58 009	TO	58 019	TO
58 010	TO		

58 020	TO	*Doncaster Works*

58 021	TO	58 028	TO
58 022	TO	58 029	TO
58 023	TO	58 030	TO
58 024	TO	58 031	TO
58 025	TO	58 032	TO
58 026	TO	58 033	TO
58 027	TO		

58 034	TO	*Bassetlaw*		
58 035	TO		58 037	TO
58 036	TO		58 038	TO
58 039	TO	*Rugeley Power Station*		
58 040	TO	*Cottam Power Station*		
58 041	TO	*Ratcliffe Power Station*		
58 042	TO	*Ironbridge Power Station*		
58 043	TO		58 047	TO
58 044	TO		58 048	TO
58 045	TO		58 049	TO
58 046	TO			
58 050	TO			

Allocation: **TO** 50 (**50**)

Class 59

Built: General Motors, USA, 1985
Engine: GM 645E3C 16-cyl of 3,300hp (2,460kW)
Weight: 126 tonnes
Brake force: 69 tonnes
Maximum tractive effort:
Route availability:
Maximum speed: 60mph
Train brakes: Air
Fuel: 990gal
Train heat: Not equipped
Equipped for one man operation. Headlights fitted
†59 001 carries a bell on the front of No 1 end cab

Owned and operated by Foster Yeoman, maintained at Merehead by Bristol (BR) staff

59 001†	HQ (BR)	*Yeoman Endeavour*
59 002	HQ (BR)	*Yeoman Enterprise*
59 003	HQ (BR)	*Yeoman Highlander*
59 004	HQ (BR)	*Yeoman Challenger*

Allocation: **HQ (BR)**4 (**4**)

Class 58 Co-Co No 58 001 stabled at Bescot holding sidings on 19 April 1986. Note Toton depot's Hare motif. *Paul Biggs*

Electro-Diesel Locomotives

Class 73/0 Bo-Bo

Built: BR 1962
Equipment: English Electric 4-cyl type RR 4 SRKT Mk 2 600bhp diesel engine; four English Electric EE 542A traction motors
Total hp: Electric 1,420 (1,060kW). Diesel 600 (447kW)
Weight: 76 tonnes
Brake force: 31 tonnes
Maximum tractive effort: Electric: 42,000lb (186kn), Diesel: 34,000lb (151kn)
Route availability: 6
Maximum speed: 80mph
Train brakes: All Air, Vacuum and Electro-Pneumatic
Fuel: 340gal
Train heat: Electric 675V dc, 400amps max
Train pre-heat: Electric from main generator
ETH index: 66 (electric)

73 001	M	SL	73 004		SL
73 002		SL	73 005	M	SL
73 003		SL	73 006		SL

Allocation: **SL** 6 (**6**)

Class 73/1 Bo-Bo

As class 73/0 except:
Built: English Electric 1965-67
Traction motors: Four English Electric EE 546/1B
Weight: 77 tonnes
Maximum tractive effort: Electric: 40,000lb (179kN), Diesel: 36,000lb (160kN)
Maximum speed: 90mph
Fuel: 310gal
Train pre-heat: Not equipped
ETH index: 66 (electric)
All equipped with flash guards for operation on Gatwick Express services.

73 101	M	SL	*Brighton Evening Argus*
73 102		SL	*Airtour Suisse*

73 103		SL	73 108		SL
73 104	M	SL	73 109		SL
73 105	M	SL	73 110		SL
73 106		SL	73 111	M	SL
73 107	M	SL	73 112		SL

73 113	M	SL	*County of West Sussex*
73 114	M	SL	
73 116	M	SL	*Selhurst*

73 117		SL	73 118		SL

73 119		SL	*Kentish Mercury*
73 120	M	SL	
73 121	M	SL	*Croydon 1883-1983*
73 122	M	SL	*County of East Sussex*
73 123		SL	*Gatwick Express*
73 124		SL	
73 125		SL	*Stewarts Lane 1860-1985*

73 126	M	SL	73 128	M	SL
73 127		SL			

73 129	M	SL	*City of Winchester*

73 130		SL	73 132	M	SL
73 131	M	SL	73 133	M	SL

73 134		SL	*Woking Homes 1885-1985*

73 135		SL	73 136		SL

73 137	M	SL	*Royal Observer Corps*

73 138	M	SL	73 140		SL
73 139		SL	73 141	M	SL

73 142	M	SL	*Broadlands*

Allocation: **SL** 41 (**41**)

AC Electric Locomotives Supply System 25kV Overhead

Class 81 Bo-Bo

Built: BRCW 1960-64
Equipment: Four AEI (BTH) 189 spring-borne dc traction motors driving through Alsthom quill drive. 3,200hp (2,387kW) continuous rating
Control system: LT Tap changing
Weight: 79 tonnes
Brake force: 40 tonnes
Maximum tractive effort: 50,000lb (222kN)
Route availability: 6
Maximum speed: 100mph (†temporarily 80mph)
Train brakes: All dual
ETH index: 66
All equipped for one-man operation

81 002	GW	81 011	GW
81 003	GW (Su KD)	81 012†	GW
81 004†	GW	81 013	GW
81 005	GW	81 014†	GW
81 006	GW	81 017	GW
81 007	GW	81 019†	GW
81 008†	GW	81 020	GW
81 009	GW	81 021	GW
81 010†	GW	81 022	GW

Allocation: **GW** 17, **Stored** 1 **(18)**

Class 82 Bo-Bo

Built: AEI (Metropolitan Vickers) 1960-61
Equipment: Four AEI 189 dc traction motors driving through Alsthom quill drive. 3,300hp continuous (2,462kW) rating
Control system: HT Tap changing
Weight: 80 tonnes
Brake force: 38 tonnes
Maximum tractive effort: 50,000lb (222kN)
Route availability: 6
Maximum speed: 40mph
ETH index: 66
Train brakes: Both Dual
One man operation: Both equipped
Radio (Cab/Shore) fitted: 82008
Special livery: *InterCity* 82008

82 005	WN	82 008	WN

Allocation: **WN** 2 **(2)**

Class 83 Bo-Bo

Built: English Electric 1961
Equipment: English Electric 535A spring-borne dc traction motors driving through SLM resilient drives. 2,950hp (2,200kW) continuous rating
Control system: LT Tap changing
Weight: 77 tonnes
Brake force: 38 tonnes
Maximum tractive effort: 38,000lb (169kN)
Route availability: 6
Maximum speed: 40mph
ETH index: 66
Train brakes: All Dual
One man operation: All equipped
Special livery: *InterCity* 83012

83 009	WN	83 015	WN
83 012	WN		

Allocation: **WN** 3 **(3)**

Class 85 Bo-Bo

Built: British Rail 1961-64
Equipment: Four AEI (BTH) 189 dc traction motors driving through Alsthom quill drive, 3,200hp (2,387kW) continuous rating
Control system: LT Tap changing
Weight: 83 tonnes
Brake force: 41 tonnes
Maximum tractive effort: 50,000lb (222kN)
Route availability: 6

Class 73/0 Bo-Bo No 73 003 passes Gillingham with the 17.16 Gillingham-London Bridge parcels train on 6 October 1986. *John Scrace*

Maximum speed: 100mph (†temporaly 80mph)
ETH index: 66
Train brakes: All Dual
Locomotive brakes: Air and Rheostatic
One man operation: All equipped

85 002	CE	85 021	CE
85 003	CE	85 022	CE
85 004	CE	85 023	CE
85 005	CE	85 024	CE
85 006	CE	85 025	CE
85 007 †	CE	85 026 †	CE
85 008 †	CE	85 028	CE
85 009 †	CE	85 029	CE
85 010 †	CE	85 030 †	CE
85 011	CE	85 031 †	CE
85 012	CE	85 032 †	CE
85 013	CE	85 034	CE
85 014	CE	85 035	CE
85 015	CE	85 036	CE
85 016	CE	85 037 †	CE
85 017	CE	85 038	CE
85 018	CE	85 039	CE
85 019	CE	85 040	CE
85 020	CE		

Allocation: **CE** 37 (**37**)

Class 86/0 Bo-Bo

Built: English Electric 1965
Equipment: EE/AEI. Four AEI type 282AZ nose-suspended traction motors. 4,040hp (3,014kW) continuous rating
Control system: HT Tap changing
Weight: 83 tonnes
Brake force: 40 tonnes
Maximum tractive effort: 58,000lb (258kN)
Route availability: 6
Maximum speed: 80mph
ETH index: 66
Train brakes: Dual
Locomotives brakes: Air and Dynamic
Multiple working: Not fitted
One-man operation: Equipped

86 007 WN

Allocation: **WN** 1 (**1**)

Class 86/1 Bo-Bo

Built: English Electric 1965-66 as Class 86
Equipment: Modified 1972 with BP9 bogies and four spring-borne GEC G412AZ traction motors and Flexicoil suspension. 5,000hp (3,730kW) continuous rating
Control System: HT Tap changing
Weight: 87 tonnes
Brake force: 40 tonnes
Maximum tractive effort: 58,000lb
Route availabilty: 6
Maximum speed: 110mph
ETH index: 66
Train brakes: All dual
Locomotive brakes: Air, Rheostatic and Dynamic
One-man operation: All equipped

86 101 L	WN	*Sir William A. Stanier FRS*
86 102	WN	*Robert A. Riddles*
86 103 L	WN	*André Chapelon*

Allocation: **WN** 3 (**3**)

Class 86/2 Bo-Bo

Built: BR Doncaster (86 205/09/14/21/22/24/27/29/31/32/36/38/40/41/42/48/52/53/56-59/61) and English Electric 1965-66
Equipment: EE/AEI. Four AEI type 282 AZ nose suspended traction motors. Modified 1972 with Flexicoil suspension, SAB resilient wheels and four AEI type 282BZ traction motors. 4,040hp (3,014kW) continuous rating

Control System: HT Tap changing
Brake force: 40 tonnes
Maximum tractive effort: 58,000lb
Route availability: 6
Train brakes: All dual
Locomotive brakes: Air and Dynamic
Weight: 85 tonnes (86 tonnes with ballast weights)
Maximum speed: 110mph (86 209/24/25/31), 100mph (others)
Ballast weights: 86 205/06/08-13/19-24/31/34-37/40/42/43/45/46/47/50/51/53-60
One-man operation: All equipped

86 204		WN	*City of Carlisle*
86 205		WN	*City of Lancaster*
86 206	L	WN	*City of Stoke on Trent*
86 207		WN	*City of Lichfield*
86 208		WN	*City of Chester*
86 209	L	WN	*City of Coventry*
86 210	L	WN	*City of Edinburgh*
86 212		WN	*Preston Guild*
86 213	L	WN	*Lancashire Witch*
86 214	L	WN	*Sans Pareil*
86 215		WN	*Joseph Chamberlain*
86 216	L	WN	*Meteor*
86 217		WN	*Halley's Comet*
86 218		WN	*Planet*
86 219		WN	*Phoenix*
86 220		WN	*Goliath*
86 221		WN	*Vesta*
86 222		WN	*Fury*
86 223		WN	*Hector*
86 224		WN	*Caledonian*
86 225	L	WN	*Hardwicke*
86 226		WN	*Royal Mail Midlands*
86 227		WN	*Sir Henry Johnson*
86 228		WN	*Vulcan Heritage*
86 229		WN	*Sir John Betjeman*
86 230	L	WN	*The Duke of Wellington*
86 231	L	WN	*Starlight Express*
86 232		WN	*Harold Macmillan*
86 233		WN	*Laurence Olivier*
86 234		WN	*J. B. Priestley OM*
86 235		WN	*Novelty*
86 236		WN	*Josiah Wedgwood*
86 237		WN	*Sir Charles Hallé*
86 238		WN	*European Community*
86 239		WN	*L. S. Lowry*
86 240		WN	*Bishop Eric Treacy*
86 241		WN	*Glenfiddich*
86 242		WN	*James Kennedy GC*
86 243		WN	*The Boys' Brigade*
86 244		WN	*The Royal British Legion*
86 245	L	WN	*Dudley Castle*
86 246		WN	*Royal Anglian Regiment*
86 247		WN	*Abraham Darby*
86 248	G	WN	*Sir Clwyd-County of Clwyd*
86 249		WN	*County of Merseyside*
86 250	L	WN	*The Glasgow Herald*
86 251		WN	*The Birmingham Post*
86 252		WN	*The Liverpool Daily Post*
86 253		WN	*The Manchester Guardian*
86 254		WN	*William Webb Ellis*
86 255		WN	*Penrith Beacon*
86 256	G	WN	*Pebble Mill*
86 257		WN	*Snowdon*
86 258		WN	*Talyllyn*
86 259		WN	*Peter Pan*
86 260		WN	*Driver Wallace Oakes GC*
86 261		WN	*Driver John Axon GC*

Allocation: **WN** 57 (**57**)

Class 86/4 Bo-Bo

Converted from Classes 86/0 and 86/3, revising third digit of number
Built: BR Doncaster (86 403/04/06/09/10/12/13/15/16/19/20/24/27/30/35/37/38) and English Electric 1965-66
Equipment: EE/AEI. Four AEI type 282 AZ nose suspended traction motors. 4,040hp (3,014kW) continuous rating
Class 86/0 and 86/3 locomotives modified from 1984 with Flexicoil suspension and SAB wheels
Control system: HT Tap changing
Maximum tractive effort: 58,000lb (258kN)
Route availability: 6
Maximum speed: 100mph
ETH index: 66
Train brakes: All Dual
Locomotive brakes: Air and Dynamic
Brake force: 40 tonnes
Ballast weights: 86 401/13/14/15/17/21/23/26/29/31/32/34-37/39

Multiple working: All fitted
One-man operation: All equipped
Special livery: *Network SouthEast:* 86 401

86 401	L	WN	
86 402		WN	
86 403	GL	WN	
86 404	L	WN	
86 405		WN	
86 406	G	WN	
86 407			
86 408	GL	WN	
86 409	L	WN	
86 410	GL	WN	
86 411		WN	*Airey Neave*
86 412	GL	WN	*Elizabeth Garrett Anderson*
86 413	L	WN	*County of Lancashire*
86 414	GL	WN	*Frank Hornby*
86 415		WN	*Rotary International*
86 416	L	WN	*Wigan Pier*
86 417		WN	*The Kingsman*
86 418	G	WN	
86 419		WN	
86 420	G	WN	
86 421	L	WN	*London School of Economics*
86 422		WN	
86 423	L	WN	
86 424	L	WN	
86 425		WN	
86 426	GL	WN	
86 427	GL	WN	*The Industrial Society*
86 428		WN	*Aldaniti*
86 430	L	WN	
86 431		WN	
86 432	G	WN	
86 433		WN	*Wulfruna*
86 434		WN	*University of London*
86 435		WN	
86 436		WN	
86 437		WN	
86 438	L	WN	
86 439	L	WN	

Allocation: **WN** 37 **(37)**

Class 87/0 Bo-Bo

Built: BREL 1973-74
Equipment: GEC Four G412AZ traction motors with flexible drive. 5,000hp (3,730kW) continuous rating
Control system: HT Tap changing
Weight: 83 tonnes
Brake force: 40 tonnes
Maximum tractive effort: 58,000lb (258kN)
Route availability: 6
Maximum speed: 110mph
ETH index: 95
Train brakes: Air
Locomotive brakes: Air, Rheostatic and Dynamic
Multiple working: All equipped
One man operation: All equipped
Driver-Guard communication fitted: All except 87004/09/14

87 001	WN	*Royal Scot*
87 002	WN	*Royal Sovereign*
87 003	WN	*Patriot*
87 004	WN	*Britannia*
87 005	WN	*City of London*
87 006	WN	*City of Glasgow*
87 007	WN	*City of Manchester*
87 008	WN	*City of Liverpool*
87 009	WN	*City of Birmingham*
87 010	WN	*King Arthur*
87 011	WN	*The Black Prince*
87 012	WN	*[Coeur de Lion]*
87 013	WN	*John O' Gaunt*
87 014	WN	*Knight of the Thistle*
87 015	WN	*Howard of Effingham*
87 016	WN	*Sir Francis Drake*
87 017	WN	*Iron Duke*

Class 81 Bo-Bo No 81 013 crosses the M6 south of Penrith with the 09.45 Blackpool-Stranraer Harbour service on 9 August 1986. *C. L. Shaw*

87 018	WN	*Lord Nelson*
87 019	WN	*Sir Winston Churchill*
87 020	WN	*North Briton*
87 021	WN	*Robert the Bruce*
87 022	WN	*Cock o' the North*
87 023	WN	*Velocity*
87 024	WN	*Lord of the Isles*
87 025	WN	*County of Cheshire*
87 026	WN	*Sir Richard Arkwright*
87 027	WN	*Wolf of Badenoch*
87 028	WN	*Lord President*
87 029	WN	*Earl Marischal*
87 030	WN	*Black Douglas*
87 031	WN	*Hal o' the Wynd*
87 032	WN	*Kenilworth*
87 033	WN	*Thane of Fife*
87 034	WN	*William Shakespeare*
87 035	WN	*Robert Burns*

Allocation: **WN** 35 **(35)**

Class 87/1 Bo-Bo

As Class 87/0 except:
Built: BREL 1975
Equipment: GEC Four G412 BZ traction motors with flexible drive. 4,850hp (3,628kW) continuous rating
Control system: Thyristor
Weight: 79 tonnes
Maximum speed: 100mph
One man operation: Equipped

87 101	HQ (HE)	*Stephenson*

Allocation: **HQ (HE)** 1 **(1)**

Class 87/2 Bo-Bo

To be introduced 1987
Built: BREL Crewe
Equipment: GEC
Control system:
Weight:
Brake force:
Maximum tractive effort:
Maximum speed: 110mph
ETH index:
Train brakes: Air
Multiple working:
One man operation:

87 201	87 217
87 202	87 218
87 203	87 219
87 204	87 220
87 205	87 221
87 206	87 222
87 207	87 223
87 208	87 224
87 209	87 225
87 210	87 226
87 211	87 227
87 212	87 228
87 213	87 229
87 214	87 230
87 215	87 231
87 216	

Allocation:

Class 89 Co-Co

Introduced 1986
Built: BREL
Equipment: Brush Traction
Control system:
Weight: 105 tonnes
Brake force:
Maximum tractive effort:
Maximum speed: 125mph
ETH index: 95
Train brakes: Air

89 001 HQ (Brush)

Allocation: **HQ** 1 (**1**)

Class 91 Bo-Bo

To be introduced 1988
Built: BREL Crewe
Equipment: GEC
Control system: Thyristor
Weight:
Brake force:
Maximum tractive effort: 6
Route availability:
Maximum speed: 125mph
ETH index:
Train brakes: Air
Multiple working:
One man operation:

91 001
91 002
91 003
91 004
91 005
91 006
91 007
91 008
91 009
91 010
91 011
91 012
91 013
91 014
91 015
91 016
91 017
91 018
91 019
91 020
91 021
91 022
91 023
91 024
91 025
91 026
91 027
91 028
91 029
91 030
91 031

Allocation:

Class 87/0 Bo-Bo No 87 001 *Royal Scot* powers its way through Crewe on 9 August 1986. *Stephen Turner*

Inter-City 125 (High Speed Train)

Classes 253 and 254

Each unit consists of a rake of seven, eight or nine Mk III coaches with a lightweight power car at each end. The units can be easily remarshalled as required.

Power cars on all Regions are now fully interchangeable, but trailer sets are maintained whenever possible in fixed formations. Current normal formations are listed at the end of this section.

Class 43 Power Car (GB5.03 DM† or DMB GB5.02)

Built: BREL 1976-7 for Western Region London-Bristol/South Wales services, 1977 for East Coast main line services, 1979-80 for West of England services and 1981-82 for North-East-South-West Services.

Engine: All fitted Paxman Valenta 12-cyl 12RP200L V-type of 2,250bhp (1,680kW) except Nos 43167/68 experimentally fitted with Mirrlees MB190 engines

Weight: 69 tonnes

Maximum tractive effort: 17,980lb (80kN)

Power/control equipment: Four Brush TMH 68-46 (43 002-055/161-198) Four GEC G417AZ (43125-151) traction motors, frame mounted

Maximum speed: 125mph

One man operation: 43163-92 equipped

† No guard's accommodation

‡ Modified exhaust manifold

§ Temporaly derated to 2,000hp (1,492kW)

43002 † OO *Top of the Pops*

43003 †	OO	43008 †	LA
43004 †	OO	43009 †	LA
43005	OO	43010 †	LA
43006	OO	43011 †	LA
43007	OO	43012 †	PM

43013 † PM *University of Bristol*

43014 †	PM	43020 †	LA
43015 †	PM	43021	LA
43016 †	PM	43022 †	LA
43017 †	PM	43023 †	LA
43018	PM	43024 †	LA
43019 †	PM	43025 †	LA

43026 † LA *City of Westminster*
43027 † LA *Westminster Abbey*

43028 †	LA	43033 †	PM
43029 †	LA	43034 †	PM
43030 †	PM	43035 †	PM
43031 †	PM	43036	PM
43032 †	PM	43037 †	PM

43038 † NL *National Railway Museum — The First Ten Years 1975-1985*

43039 †‡	NL	43042‡	BN
43040 †	BN	43043 †	BN
43041 †‡	BN	43044	NL

43045 † NL *The Grammar School Doncaster AD 1350*

43046 † NL

43047 † NL *Rotherham Enterprise*

43048 † NL

43049 † NL *Neville Hill*

43050 † NL 43051 † NL

43052 NL *City of Peterborough*
43053‡ NL *County of Humberside*

43054 † NL 43055 † NL

43056 †‡ BN *University of Bradford*
43057 † BN *Bounds Green*

43058 HT 43059 † HT

43060 §	NL	*County of Leicestershire*	
43061 †	NL	*City of Lincoln*	
43062 †‡	BN	43063 †	BN
43064 †‡	NL	*City of York*	
43065 †	NL	43071 †	NL
43066 †	NL	43072 †	NL
43067 †‡	NL	43073 †	NL
43068 †	NL	43074 †	BN
43069 †‡	NL	43075 †	BN
43070	NL	43076 †‡	NL
43077	NL	*County of Nottingham*	
43078	HT	*Shildon, County Durham*	
43079 ‡	HT	43082	BN
43080	BN	43083	BN
43081	BN		
43084 ‡	BN	*County of Derbyshire*	
43085	BN	*City of Bradford*	
43086 §	EC	43087	EC
43088 †	EC	*XIII Commonwealth Games, Edinburgh 1986*	
43089	EC	43090 ‡	EC
43091	EC	*Edinburgh Military Tattoo*	
43092 ‡	EC	*Highland Chieftain*	
43093	EC	43094 †	HT
43095	HT	*Heaton*	
43096	HT	*The Queen's Own Hussars*	
43097	HT	*The Light Infantry*	
43098 ‡	HT	*Tyne and Wear Metropolitan County*	
43099 ‡	HT		
43100	EC	*Craigentinny*	
43101	EC	*Edinburgh International Festival*	
43102 †	HT	*City of Wakefield*	
43103 †	HT		

43104	HT	*County of Cleveland*	
43105 †	HT	*Hartlepool*	
43106	BN		
43107	BN	*City of Derby*	
43108	NL	43109	NL
43110‡	HT	*Darlington*	
43111 †	HT	43112 ‡	HT
43113	HT	*City of Newcastle-upon-Tyne*	
43114	BN	43115 ‡	BN
43116	NL	*City of Kingston-upon-Hull*	
43117	NL	43119	NL
43118	NL	43120 †	NL
43121 †	NL	*West Yorkshire Metropolitan County*	
43122	NL	*South Yorkshire Metropolitan County*	
43123	BN		
43124 †	PM	*BBC Points West*	
43125	PM	*Merchant Venturer*	
43126	PM	*City of Bristol*	
43127 †	PM	43129	PM
43128 †	PM	43130	PM
43131	PM	*Sir Felix Pole*	
43132 †	PM	43137	OO
43133	PM	43138	OO
43134	PM	43139	OO
43135	PM	43140	OO
43136	PM	43141 †	OO
43142 †	OO	*St Mary's Hospital, Paddington*	
43143 †	OO	43144 †	OO

43145	OO	43149 †	OO
43146 †	OO	43150 †	OO
43147	OO	43151 †	PM
43148	OO		
43152	NL	*St Peters School York AD 627*	
43153 †	NL	*University of Durham*	
43154 †§	NL	43156 †	NL
43155 †	NL		
43157 †‡	NL	*Yorkshire Evening Post*	
43158 †	NL	43160 †‡	NL
43159 †	NL	43161 †	NL
43162 †	NL	*Borough of Stevenage*	
43163 †	LA	43176 †	PM
43164 †	LA	43177 †	PM
43165 †	LA	43178 †	LA
43166 †	LA	43179 †‡	HT
43167 †	PM	43180 †	OO
43168 †	PM	43181 †	LA
43169 †	PM	43182 †‡	NL
43170 †	PM	43183 †	LA
43171 †	PM	43184 †	LA
43172 †	PM	43185 †	LA
43173 †	PM	43186 †	LA
43174 †	PM	43187 †	LA
43175 †	PM		
43188 †	LA	*City of Plymouth*	
43189 †	LA	43191 †	LA
43190 †	LA	43192 †	LA
43193 †‡	NL	*Yorkshire Post*	
43194 †	NL	*Royal Signals*	
43195 †	NL		
43196 †	NL	*The Newspaper Society*	
43197 †	NL	43198 †	NL

Allocations: **BN** 21, **HT** 19, **NL** 55
EC 10
LA 30, **OO** 21, **PM** 41 **(197)**

InterCity 125 Trailers

Trailer Restaurant Buffet TRB GN4.01
Body: 75′ 3″×9′ 1″ (22.93×2.76mm)
Seats: Unclassified, 23
Weight: 36 tonnes

40204	OO	40209	OO
40205	PM	40210	OO
40206	PM	40211	OO
40207	PM	40212	OO
40208	PM	40213	OO

Allocations: **OO** 6, **PM** 4 **(10**

Trailer Restaurant Unclassed Buffet TRUB GK4.01
Body: 75′ 3″×9′ 1″ (22.93×2.76m)
Seats: 17
Weight: 38 tonnes

40322	LA	40327	LA
40323	LA	40331	LA
40324	LA	40332	LA
40325	LA	40355	LA
40326	LA	40357	LA

Allocation: **LA** 10 **(10**

Trailer Restaurant Second Buffet TRSB GK2.02
Body: 75′ 3″×9′ 1″ (22.93×2.76m)
Seats: 2nd, 35
Weight: 36 tonnes

40401	PM	40423	OO
40402	PM	40424	OO
40403	PM	40425	PM
40414	PM	40426	LA
40415	PM	40427	OO
40416	OO	40428	OO
40417	PM	40429	PM
40418	PM	40430	PM
40419	PM	40431	LA
40420	PM	40432	LA
40421	PM	40433	LA
40422	PM	40434	LA

InterCity 125 set No 253 030 makes its way through unusual territory as it approaches Radwag Green Crossing while working the diverted Exeter St Davids-Manchester service on 21 September 1986. *T. R. Moors*

40435	BN	40437	PM
40436	PM		

Allocations: **BN** 1
LA 5, **OO** 5, **PM** 16 **(27)**

Trailer Restaurant First Kitchen TRFK GL1.02

Body: 75′ 3″×9′ 1″ (22.93×2.76m)
Seats: 1st, 24
Weight: 37 tonnes

40501	NL	40510	BN
40505	BN	40511	HT
40509	NL		

Allocations: **BN** 2, **HT** 2, **NL** 1 **(5)**

Trailer Restaurant Unclassed Kitched TRUK GL4.02

Body: 75′ 3″×9′ 1″ (22.93×2.76m)
Seats: 24
Weight: 37 tonnes

40512	HQ (ZN) (S)
40514	HQ (ZN) (S)
40518	HQ (ZN) (S)

Allocations: **3 stored ZN** for possible conversion to Royal Stock.

Trailer Lounge Unclassed Kitchen TLUK GM4.01

Body: 75′ 3″×9′ 1″ (22.93×2.76m)
Seats: 12
Weight: 37 tonnes
Available for special hire as additional or replacement in standard train

40513	BN

Allocation: **BN** 1 **(1)**

Trailer Restaurant First Buffet TRFB GK1.01

Body: 75′ 3″×9′ 1″ (22.93×2.76m)
Seats: 1st, 17
Weight: 38 tonnes
‡Under conversion to Modular Catering

Formerly numbered 403xx

40700		NL	40730	NL
40701		BN	40733	NL
40702		BN	40734	BN
40703		BN	40735	NL
40704		NL	40736	EC
40705		BN	40737	NL
40706		BN	40738	NL
40707		NL	40739	NL
40708		NL	40740	HT
40709		NL	40741	NL
40710		EC	40742	NL
40711		EC	40743	NL
40712		EC	40744	NL
40713		EC	40745	NL
40714		EC	40746	NL
40715		NL	40747	NL
40716		NL	40748	NL
40717		NL	40749	NL
40718		NL	40750	NL
40719	‡	BN	40751	NL
40720		BN	40752	EC
40721		NL	40753	NL
40728		EC	40754	NL
40729		NL	40756	BN

Allocations: **BN** 9, **HT** 1, **NL** 30
EC 8 **(48)**

Trailer First TF GH1.01

Body: 75′ 3″×9′ 1″ (22.93×2.76m)
Seats: 1st, 48
Toilets: 2
Weight: 33 tonnes
† Vehicles rebuilt from former Class 252 trailer vehicles

41003	OO	41007	OO
41004	OO	41008	OO
41005	OO	41009	OO
41006	OO	41010	OO
41011	PM	41059	NL

012		PM	41060		NL
013		PM	41061		NL
014		PM	41062		NL
015		PM	41063		NL
016		PM	41064		NL
017		PM	41065		NL
018		PM	41066	T	HT
019		OO	41067		NL
020		OO	41068		NL
021		OO	41069		NL
022		OO	41070		NL
023		LA	41071		EC
024		LA	41072		EC
025		LA	41073		EC
026		LA	41074		EC
027		LA	41075		BN
028		LA	41076		BN
029		LA	41077		NL
030		LA	41078		NL
031		LA	41079		NL
032		LA	41080		NL
033		LA	41081		BN
034		LA	41082		BN
035		LA	41083		BN
036		LA	41084		BN
037		LA	41085		BN
038		LA	41086		BN
039		NL	41087		BN
040		NL	41088		BN
041	T	NL	41089		BN
042		NL	41090		BN
043		NL	41091		NL
044		NL	41092		NL
045		NL	41093		NL
046		NL	41094		NL
047		NL	41095		EC
048		NL	41096		EC
049		NL	41097		EC
050		NL	41098		EC
051		NL	41099		EC
052		NL	41100		EC
053		NL	41101		EC
054		NL	41102		EC
055		NL	41103		EC
056		NL	41104		EC
057		NL	41105		EC
058		NL	41106		EC
107		NL	41142		PM

41108	NL	41143	PM
41109	NL	41144	PM
41110	NL	41145	PM
41111	NL	41146	PM
41112	NL	41147	PM
41113	NL	41148	PM
41114	NL	41149	NL
41115	BN	41150	NL
41116	BN	41151	HT
41117	BN	41152	HT
41118	BN	41153	NL
41119	NL	41154	NL
41120	NL	41155	NL
41121	LA	41156	NL
41122	LA	41157	NL
41123	PM	41158	NL
41124	PM	41159	PM
41125	LA	41160	PM
41126	LA	41161	PM
41127	PM	41162	PM
41128	PM	41163	PM
41129	PM	41164	PM
41130	PM	41165	PM
41131	PM	41166	LA
41132	PM	41167	LA
41133	OO	41168	LA
41134	OO	41169	LA
41135	OO	41170†	BN
41136	OO	41171†	BN
41137	OO	41172	BN
41138	OO	41173	BN
41139	OO	41174	BN
41140	OO	41175	NL
41141	PM	41176	NL

Allocations: **BN** 21, **HT** 3, **NL** 59
EC 16
LA 24, **OO** 20, **PM** 31 (**174**)

Trailer Second TS GH2.02 or GH2.03*
Body: 75′ 3″×9′ 1″ (22.93×2.76m)
Seats: 2nd, 72, 76*
Toilets: 2
Weight: 33 tonnes

42003	OO	42051	LA
42004	OO	42052	LA
42005	OO	42053	LA
42006	OO	42054	LA

InterCity 125 Trailers

42007	00	42055	LA
42008	00	42056	LA
42009	00	42057	NL
42010	00	42058	NL
42011	00	42059	NL
42012	00	42060	NL
42013	00	42061	NL
42014	00	42062	NL
42015	PM	42063	NL
42016	PM	42064	NL
42017	PM	42065	NL
42018	PM	42066	NL
42019	PM	42067	NL
42020	PM	42068	NL
42021	PM	42069	NL
42022	PM	42070	NL
42023	PM	42071	NL
42024	PM	42072	NL
42025	PM	42073	NL
42026	PM	42074	NL
42027	00	42075 *	NL
42028	00	42076	NL
42029	00	42077	NL
42030	00	42078 *	NL
42031	00	42079	NL
42032	00	42080	NL
42033	LA	42081	NL
42034	LA	42082	NL
42035	LA	42083	NL
42036	LA	42084	PM
42037	LA	42085	PM
42038	LA	42086	PM
42039	LA	42087	PM
42040	LA	42088	PM
42041	LA	42089	PM
42042	LA	42090	PM
42043	LA	42091	PM
42044	LA	42092	PM
42045	LA	42093	PM
42046	LA	42094	PM
42047	LA	42095	PM
42048	LA	42096	LA
42049	LA	42097	LA
42050	LA	42098	LA

42099	LA	42149 *	BN
42100 *	NL	42150	NL
42101 *	BN	42151	NL
42102 *	BN	42152	NL
42103 *	BN	42153	NL
42104	BN	42154	NL
42105 *	BN	42155 *	NL
42106	NL	42156 *	NL
42107	NL	42157 *	NL
42108	PM	42158 *	NL
42109	PM	42159 *	BN
42110	PM	42160 *	BN
42111	NL	42161 *	BN
42112	NL	42162 *	NL
42113	NL	42163 *	BN
42115	NL	42164 *	BN
42116	NL	42165 *	BN
42117	NL	42166 *	NL
42118	NL	42167 *	BN
42119	NL	42168 *	BN
42120	NL	42169 *	BN
42121	NL	42170 *	NL
42122	BN	42171	BN
42123 *	NL	42172	BN
42124 *	NL	42173	BN
42125 *	NL	42174 *	NL
42126	NL	42175 *	BN
42127	BN	42176 *	BN
42128	BN	42177 *	BN
42129	NL	42178 *	BN
42130	BN	42179	NL
42131	NL	42180	NL
42132	NL	42181	NL
42133	NL	42182 *	HT
42134	BN	42183	NL
42135	NL	42184	NL
42136	NL	42185	NL
42137	NL	42186 *	HT
42138	BN	42187	EC
42139 *	EC	42188	EC
42140 *	EC	42189	EC
42141 *	EC	42190 *	HT
42143	EC	42191 *	EC
42144	EC	42192	EC
42145	EC	42193	EC
42146	NL	42194	EC
42147 *	BN	42195 *	NL
42148 *	BN	42196 *	EC

An InterCity 125 set approaches Leicester on 15 June 1986 with the 16.30 Nottingham-London St Pancras service. This scene has been transformed with the Leicester Gap Resignalling scheme. *Paul A. Biggs*

InterCity 125 Trailers

No.	Depot
42197	EC
42198	EC
42199	EC
42200 *	NL
42201	EC
42202	EC
42203	EC
42204	EC
42205 *	NL
42206	EC
42207	EC
42208	EC
42209	EC
42210 *	NL
42211 *	EC
42212	EC
42213	EC
42214	EC
42215	NL
42216 *	LA
42217	NL
42218	NL
42219	NL
42220	NL
42221 *	LA
42222	NL
42223	NL
42224	NL
42225	NL
42226	NL
42227	NL
42228	NL
42229	NL
42230	NL
42231	NL
42232	NL
42233	NL
42234	NL
42235	NL
42236	NL
42237 *	BN
42238 *	BN
42239 *	BN
42240	NL
42241 *	BN
42242	BN
42243	BN
42244	BN
42245	NL
42246 *	NL
42247 *	NL
42248 *	NL
42249 *	NL
42250	NL
42251 *	LA
42252 *	LA
42253 *	LA
42254	PM
42255	PM
42256	PM
42257	PM
42258	PM
42259 *	LA
42260 *	LA
42261 *	LA
42262	PM
42263	PM
42264	PM
42265	PM
42266	PM
42267	PM
42268	PM
42269	PM
42270	PM
42271	PM
42272	PM
42273	PM
42274	PM
42275	OO
42276	OO
42277	PM
42278	PM
42279 *	OO
42280 *	OO
42281 *	OO
42282	PM
42283	OO
42284	OO
42285	OO
42286	PM
42287	OO
42288	OO
42289	OO
42290	PM
42291	PM
42292	PM
42293	PM
42294	PM
42295	PM
42296	PM
42297	PM
42298	PM
42299	PM
42300	PM
42301	PM
42302	PM
42303	PM
42304	PM
42305	PM
42306	LA
42307	LA
42308	LA
42309	LA
42310	LA
42311	LA
42312	LA
42313	LA
42314	LA
42315	LA
42316	LA
42317	LA
42318	LA
42319	LA
42320	LA
42321	LA
42322	PM
42323 *	NL
42324 *	NL
42325 *	NL
42326 *	EC
42327 *	BN
42328 *	NL
42329 *	EC
42330 *	BN
42331 *	NL
42332 *	NL
42333 *	EC
42334 *	NL
42335 *	NL
42336 *	NL
42337 *	NL
42338 *	BN
42339 *	NL
42340 *	NL
42341 *	NL
42342 (44082) *	LA
42343 (44095) *	LA
42344 (44092) *	LA
42345 (44096) *	LA

Allocations: **BN** 39, **HT** 3, **NL** 112
EC 31
LA 54, **OO** 30, **PM** 65 **(324**

Trailer Guard Second TGS GJ2.01
Body: 75′ 3″×9′ 1″ (22.93×2.76m)
Seats: 2nd, 63
Toilet: 1
Weight: 33 tonnes

No.	Depot
44000	PM
44001	OO
44002	OO
44003	OO
44004	OO
44005	PM
44006	PM
44007	PM
44008	PM
44009	OO
44010	OO
44011	LA
44012	OO
44013	OO
44014	OO
44015	LA

44016	LA	44038	PM	44061	EC	44080	HT
44017	LA	44039	PM	44062	PM	44081	PM
44018	LA	44040	PM	44063	EC	44083	NL
44019	NL	44041	NL	44064	EC	44084	LA
44020	NL	44042	NL	44065	PM	44085	NL
44021	NL	44043	NL	44066	HT	44086	NL
44022	NL	44044	NL	44067	HT	44087	PM
44023	NL	44045	BN	44068	PM	44088	LA
44024	NL	44046	NL	44069	PM	44089	LA
44025	NL	44047	NL	44070	NL	44090	LA
44026	NL	44048	EC	44071	NL	44091	LA
44027	NL	44049	EC	44072	PM	44093	BN
44028	LA	44050	BN	44073	NL	44094	NL
44029	PM	44051	NL	44074	NL	44097	HT
44030	LA	44052	NL	44075	BN	44098	EC
44031	PM	44053	BN	44076	PM	44099	OO
44032	PM	44054	BN	44077	BN	44100	NL
44033	PM	44055	BN	44078	NL	44101	NL
44034	OO	44056	BN				
44035	OO	44057	BN				
44036	OO	44058	NL				
44037	OO	44059	NL				
44060	HT	44079	NL				

Allocations: **BN** 10, **HT** 5, **NL** 31
EC 6
LA 12,
OO 14, **PM** 20 (**98**)

n InterCity 125 set forms the 09.15 Exeter-Manchester service and is seen here at tafford station. *John Gosling*

InterCity 125 Formations

EAST COAST MAIN LINE IC125 TRAILER CAR FORMATIONS

Unit	Allocation	TF	TF	TRFB/ TRFK	TF	TS/ TRFB	TS	TS	TS	TGS
254 001 R	NL	41057	41058	40708	—	42335	42111	42112	42113	44041
254 002 R	NL	41059	41060	40733	—	42336	42115	42116	42117	44042
254 003 R	NL	41061	41062	40729	—	42337	42119	42120	42121	44043
254 004 R	NL	41063	41064	40754	—	42328	42123	42124	42125	44044
254 005 R	BN	41171	41173	40734	—	42338	42178	42127	42128	44045
254 006	NL	41067	41068	40730	—	42331	42131	42132	42133	44046
254 007 R	NL	41069	41070	40751	—	42339	42135	42136	42137	44047
254 008 R	EC	41071	41072	40728	—	42329	42139	42140	42141	44048
254 009	EC	41073	41074	40752	—	42333	42143	42144	42145	44049
254 010 R	BN	41075	41076	40756	—	42327	42147	42148	42149	44050
254 011	NL	41077	41078	40753	—	42324	42151	42152	42153	44051
254 012 R	NL	41079	41080	40700	—	42155	42156	42157	42100	44052
254 013 R	BN	41081	41082	40701	—	42159	42160	42161	42101	44053
254 014 R	BN	41083	41084	40702	—	42163	42164	42165	42102	44054
254 015 R	BN	41085	41086	40703	—	42169	42168	42167	42103	44055
254 016 R	BN	41087	41088	40706	—	42171	42172	42173	42104	44056
254 017 R	BN	41089	41090	40705	—	42175	42176	42177	42105	44057
254 018 R	NL	41091	41092	40704	—	42179	42180	42181	42106	44058
254 019 R	NL	41093	41094	40707	—	42183	42184	42185	42107	44059
254 020	EC	41095	41096	40736	—	42326	42187	42188	42189	44060
254 021	EC	41097	41098	40710	—	42191	42192	42193	42194	44061
254 022	EC	41099	41100	40711	—	42196	42197	42198	42199	44063
254 023	EC	41101	41102	40712	—	42201	42202	42203	42204	44064
254 024	EC	41103	41104	40713	—	42206	42207	42208	42209	44066
254 025	EC	41105	41106	40714	—	42211	42212	42213	42214	44067
254 026	NL	41107	41108	40715	—	42341 R	42217	42218	42219	44070
254 027	NL	41109	41110	40716	—	42334	42222	42223	42224	44071
254 028	NL	41111	41112	40749	—	42226	42227	42228	42229	44073
254 029	NL	41113	41114	40718	—	42231	42232	42233	42234	44074
254 030 R	BN	41115	41116	40742	—	42330	42237	42238	42239	44075
254 031	BN	41117	41118	40720	—	42241	42242	42243	42244	44077
254 032 R	NL	41119	41120	40721	—	42246	42247	42248	42249	44078
254 033 R	NL	41149	41150	40739	—	42162	42166	42170	42174	44079
254 034 R	HT (PUL)	41151	41066	40511 K	41152	40740 B	42186	42190	42182	44080
254 035	NL	41153	41154	40741	—	42195	42200	42205	42210	44083
254 036	NL	41155	41156	40748	—	42215	42220	42225	42230	44085
254 037	NL	41157	41158	40743	—	42235	42240	42245	42250	44086
254 038 R	NL	41055	41056	40709	—	42081	42082	42083	42126	44027
254 039 R	NL	41045	41065	40738	—	42062	42066	42067	42068	44022
254 040	NL	41047	41048	40744	—	42069	42070	42071	42118	44023
254 041 R	NL	41049	41050	40745	—	42325	42072	42073	42074	44024
254 042 R	NL	41051	41052	40746	—	42078	42075	42076	42077	44025
254 043	NL	41053	41054	40747	—	42332	42236	42079	42080	44026
254 044	BN	41174	41172	40435 (TRSB)	—	42130	42134	42138	42122	44093
254 045	NL	41176	41175	40750	—	42158	42146	42150	42154	44094

254 046	NL	41039	41040	40735	—	42323	42057	42058	42059	44019
254 047 R	NL (PUL)	41042	41041	40501 K	41046	40717 B	42060	42061	—	44020
254 048 R	NL	41043	41044	40737	—	42340	42063	42064	42065	44021

Spare TRFB 40719 (under conversion to Modular Catering for Sheffield Pullman)
TS 42129
TLUK R 40513
TRFK 40505, 40509, 40510
TF R 41170
TGS 44097, 44098, 44100, 44101

R: Refurbished sets or vehicle
PUL: Sets for Tees-Tyne and Yorkshire Pullman services

WESTERN REGION IC125 TRAILER CAR FORMATIONS

Unit	Allocation	TF	TF	TRB	TS	TS	TS	TGS
253 001	OO	41003	41004	40209	42003	42004	42005	44001
253 002	OO	41005	41006	40212	42006	42007	42008	44002
253 003	OO	41007	41008	40213	42009	42010	42011	44003
253 004	OO	41009	41010	40204	42012	42013	42014	44004
253 005	PM	41011	41012	40205	42015	42016	42017	44005
253 006	PM	41013	41014	40206	42018	42019	42020	44006
253 007	PM	41015	41016	40207	42021	42022	42023	44007
253 008	PM	41017	41018	40208	42024	42025	42026	44008
253 009	OO	41019	41020	40211	42027	42028	42029	44009
253 010	OO	41021	41022	40210	42030	42031	42032	44010

Unit	Allocation	TF	TF	TRUB	TS	TS	TS	TS	TGS
253 011 R	LA	41023	41024	40355	42096	42033	42034	42035	44011
253 012 R	LA	41025	41026	40323	42097	42036	42037	42038	44012
253 013 R	LA	41027	41028	40325	42098	42039	42040	42041	44013
253 014 R	LA	41029	41030	40326	42099	42042	42043	42044	44014
253 015 R	LA	41031	41032	40327	42216	42045	42046	42047	44015
253 016	LA	41033	41034	40331	42221	42048	42049	42050	44016
253 017 R	LA	41035	41036	40332	42342	42051	42052	42053	44017
253 018 R	LA	41037	41038	40357	42343	42054	42055	42056	44018

Unit	Allocation	TF	TF	TRUB/ TRSB	TS	TS	TS	TS	TGS
253 028 R	LA	41121	41122	40322	42345	42251	42252	42253	44028
253 029	PM	41123	41124	40422 S	—	42255	42256	42257	44029
253 030 R	LA	41126	41125	40324	42344	42259	42260	42261	44030
253 031	PM	41127	41128	40429 S	—	42263	42264	42265	44031
253 032	PM	41129	41130	40436 S	—	42267	42268	42269	44032
253 033	PM	41131	41132	40437 S	—	42271	42272	42273	44033
253 034	OO	41133	41134	40427 S	—	42275	42276	42277	44034
253 035	OO	41135	41136	40423 S	—	42279	42280	42281	44035
253 036	OO	41137	41138	40428 S	—	42283	42284	42285	44036

InterCity 125 Formations

253 037	00	41139	41140	40416 S	—	42287	42288	42289	44037
253 038	PM	41141	41142	40417 S	—	42291	42292	42293	44038
253 039	PM	41143	41144	40418 S	—	42295	42296	42297	44039
253 040	PM	41145	41146	40419 S	—	42299	42300	42301	44040

Unit	Allocation	TF	TRSB	TS	TS	TS	TS	TSG
253 041	PM	41147	40401	42254	42258	42262	42266	44000
253 042	PM	41148	40402	42270	42274	42278	42282	44062
253 043	PM	41159	40403	42286	42290	42294	42298	44065
253 044	PM	41160	40425	42302	42303	42304	42305	44068
253 045	PM	41161	40421	42084	42085	42086	42087	44069
253 046 R	PM	41162	40414	42088	42089	42090	42091	44072
253 047 R	PM	41163	40415	42092	42093	42094	42095	44076
253 051 R	PM	41165	40430	42108	42109	42110	42322	44087
253 052	LA	41166	40431	42306	42307	42308	42309	44088
253 053	LA	41167	40432	42310	42311	42312	42313	44089
253 054	LA	41168	40433	42314	42315	42316	42317	44090
253 055	LA	41169	40434	42318	42319	42320	42321	44091
Spares	PM	41164	40420					44081
	00		40424					44099
	LA		40426					44084

InterCity 125 power car No 43 188 is seen on a test run before repainting on 31 March 1986, near Clay Mills just north of Burton-on-Trent. *C. J. Tuffs*